GOD'S HEART FOR GIVING

WHAT THE SCRIPTURES SAY ABOUT TITHING, GIVING AND PROSPERITY

ROZALIA GARRETT

Dedication

I dedicate this book first and foremost to the Holy Spirit who enabled me to write it. He gave me much love and passion for the Word of God, enlightened my mind to understand it, and helped me sort and organize the copious insights into an intelligible document. He deserves all the glory and credit.

Next, I dedicate this book to my dear husband and three beautiful daughters, true women of God, who ever so patiently supported me during the many years of wholehearted research and writing this book. Thank you for believing in me and encouraging me through the process!

Last, but not least, I dedicate this book to my one and only sister, Zsuzsi, who is the epitome of what *God's Heart for Giving* represents.

Acknowledgments

A special acknowledgment is due my husband who painstakingly read through many revisions till I felt it was right, and finally prepared the book for publishing. Thank you, sweetheart, for all your help and sacrifice!

I also express my deep-felt appreciation to all who read the manuscript and encouraged me to publish it, believing in the importance of its content. Thank you for sacrificing your time, offering your helpful comments and suggestions, and standing behind me!

Contents

INTRODUCTION

AWAKENING

God is a lavish giver. No greater way can one possibly demonstrate his love than by laying down his life for another. This is what God had done when He offered His only Son, Jesus Christ, to die on the cross for our sins. Astonishingly, He did this while we were still deep in sin: "while we were still sinners, Christ died for us." (Romans 5:8) If that would not have been enough, we read: "He who did not spare His own Son, but delivered Him up for us all, how shall He not with Him also freely give us all things?" (Romans 8:32). God proves to be a lavish giver.

How can we respond to this kind of generosity? Can we give back to God? How? Does He expect something in return? Created in His image and sanctified by His Holy Spirit, we carry His heart – His heart to give, and a heart for others. Giving should be a natural response. What does He desire or even require?

I believe that the most important and honoring thing we can do for God is to receive His free gifts with utmost gratitude. Receiving the gift of salvation by faith in Jesus Christ, particularly, must offer Him and all the heavenly angels the greatest joy. We might have a difficult time comprehending it, but salvation is a free gift: "For by grace you have been saved through faith, and that not of yourselves; it is the gift of God, not of works, lest anyone should boast." (Ephesians 2:8-9)

How else can we honor Him or give back to Him? The next most honoring thing we can do for God is to pass on what we have received. He has freely given, we freely receive; we freely receive, we freely give. We have received -- among many other things -- love, forgiveness, mercy and grace, honor and value, patience and joy, power and strength. Giving blesses. As we bless others, we bless and honor God.

1

The concept of giving back to God has a special meaning in Christendom today. It is often associated with paying back to God ten percent of our income, which is commonly called tithing. Some preachers teach that the tithe actually belongs to God and not paying Him is same as robbing Him. Robbing God of the tithe, they teach, results in God removing His protection over our lives – leaving non-tithers open to curses. On the other hand, paying one's tithes will cause God to open the windows of heaven and pour out such abundant blessings that the tithers will not be able to contain them.

Naturally, the responses to this teaching could be varied. If this is what the Bible teaches, one might want to do everything in their power to follow God's instructions. However, the presentation of impending curses if someone does not pay his tithes could cause alarm, confusion, fear and distress in some. In others, if they have been paying their tithes faithfully, they may wonder about the teaching if they have not experienced the promised result. What does the Bible actually teach about tithing? The inquiry calls for an in-depth study of Scripture.

My search for understanding the tithe began with a question I was wondering about: "What does the *Bible* teach about tithing? Who is it for and why?" The purpose for tithing I repeatedly heard taught was to receive God's abundant blessings and to evade the impending curse that follows non-tithers. What was it about the tithe that caused God to render such serious consequences? What was its exact purpose?

The curiosity turned into an elaborate, in-depth study of Scripture. Through it all I came away with two major conclusions. One was that the tithe cannot fully be understood outside of the whole counsel of God – that every tithing Scripture connects to another, each adding to the puzzle of complete understanding. But complete understanding is possible and once it is attained, any question can easily be answered about the tithe.

The second conclusion was a big surprise. It was the discovery that the biblical tithe has very little, if anything, to do with what we call tithing today. The two concepts of tithing are vastly different! I begged to know the answer to the question, "How can these two very different concepts be rooted in the same Scriptures and have the same name?" Are they both biblical? Are they reconcilable? After a comprehensive study of tithing – covering every Scripture in both the Old and New Testaments – the reader is invited to form his or her conclusions. The study of the tithe is covered in PART I.

Tithing is an integral part of the prosperity gospel. This gospel teaches that tithing and giving beyond the tithe lay the foundation for achieving financial prosperity. The focus of many sermons is on how to gain the most from giving, or stated in prosperity language, where to sow (such as a ministry or person), and how to sow, to bring in the greatest financial harvest. Incentivizing giving is a good thing and is biblical, but strategizing this way may foster greed and the idea that giving is about self.

Prosperity is certainly in the plans of God for us, but how it is defined in Scripture is necessary to know. What is prosperity from a biblical perspective? Is it riches and wealth? Is giving the "ways and means" to becoming financially prosperous? Are givers guaranteed prosperity (riches)? Does the New Testament promise wealth? Rewards certainly follow obedience, but are all the rewards for giving earthly? Seeking God's heart in context of Scripture from where prosperity is taught answers these and many more questions. PARTS II and III are devoted to this study.

It may be evident to the reader by now that this book is a response to a doctrine (to be described in more detail later) which I heard taught over the course of several years. Questions that had risen in me lead me to the Scriptures which then had me engaged in hundreds of hours of Bible study. This book offers my research and findings. I did not set out to write a book. I share my findings in case others are struggling with the same questions and looking for help to find the answers.

As to the method of research, some Bible scholars have stated that the best interpreter of Scripture is Scripture itself. Studying the whole counsel of God and paying attention to context is the key to understanding God's Word. *God's Heart for Giving* utilizes this understanding. Beyond diligence and method, the most important element in understanding God's Word is partnering with the Holy Spirit—the Author of this magnificent Bible and the One Who alone is able to reveal it to men.

God's Heart for Giving invites the reader on a journey with God through His Word – engaging in an in-depth study on tithing, giving and prosperity. The reader should find himself or herself be caught up in a beautiful love story and finish up with a wonderful reward: a fresh discovery of God's incomprehensible love for mankind. My prayer is that it be so.

CONFUSION OVER TITHING
Supremacy of God's Word

The Bible is a holy and a truly unique book. Penned by 40 men over the span of 1,500 years, it has one Author – the Holy Spirit. In it God expresses His thoughts on many things, and we are given the awesome privilege and responsibility of seeking Him for the meaning of the messages behind the words. "But know this first of all, that no prophecy of Scripture is a matter of one's own interpretation, for no prophecy was ever made by an act of human will, but men moved by the Holy Spirit spoke from God." (2 Peter 1:20-21, NASB) Since "All Scripture is inspired by God..." (2 Timothy 3:16a), we can conclude that interpretation of all Scripture ultimately belongs to the Holy Spirit. Only the book's Author can help us understand His mind.

In reading and teaching the Bible, our first goal should always be to preserve the purity of God's Word. The Apostle Paul says it this way: "Be diligent to present yourself approved to God, a worker who does not need to be ashamed, rightly dividing the word of truth." (2 Timothy 2:15)

Frankly, dividing the Word rightly is not easy. Even after diligent study and best efforts, interpreting Scripture can be challenging. The many doctrines derived from Scripture attest to this fact. Therefore, it is wise to always present the Word in its context, and to clarify when special interpretation or application of the passage is given. In other words, it is wise to guard against inadvertently replacing the inspired and inerrant Word with an interpretation (which is subject to error) and thereby unintentionally misrepresenting God's Word to the hearers.

Sometimes the Bible does not explicitly teach something, but we interpret it as if it does. Tithing today is one such example. Many Bible teachers see tithing passages as holding an important principle that applies to us today. This is the principle of the tenth – that the tenth of our income belongs to God. Now, this definition of the tithe – tenth of income – is nowhere found in the Bible. It is derived from the root meaning of the Hebrew word translated as "tithe" which means "tenth." Tenth is just a portion. The portion is significant, but so is what it is tenth of. Since tithing is in context of giving, the natural human deduction is that the "tithe" has to be "tenth of income" in today's culture. This is one common interpretation that has several shortcomings as will be seen later. But to its quick evaluation whether it passes God's litmus test – or heart – on giving, let us look at how this interpretation of tithing plays out in real life.

Tithing Ten Percent of Income

Tithing ten percent of income is generally perceived as fair and equitable to all. But a closer look challenges this perception. With a wide range of income levels, a closer look reveals a great discrepancy in the ability of paying one's tithes. Some can pay their tithes with breeze while others need to sacrifice basic needs to pay ten percent.

Life requires a minimum income to cover basic needs. Sometimes minimum wage does not even meet those needs, leaving no money to be able to tithe on. The more money one makes, the easier basic needs are met, and more is left over – making it easier to tithe. Interestingly, it is not only easier for the reason that there is more money, but the relative amount of the tithe decreases as the amount of income increases. Let me explain through some practical examples what I mean.

At about minimum wage of $18,000 per year a person's monthly gross income is $1500, out of which the net maybe, let's say, $1,300 per month. The tithe on $1,500 is $150. This amount likely requires sacrificing basic needs to pay out of $1,300 in today's economy, if even possible. Sadly, most commonly these low-wage earners are single mothers raising one or more children.

Now, someone making $72,000 per year grosses $6,000/month. The tithe on $6,000 is $600. Let's say the net monthly income is $4,700. Paying the tithe of $600 from this amount leaves $4,100 *spending* money. No sacrifice is required. While this person nets *$3400 more* (4700-1300) than the previous person, he tithes *only* $450 more!

The gaps only increase with greater income. If a person makes $120,000/year, or $10,000/month, let's say he nets $7,500. After tithing $1000, there is left $6,500/month *spending* money! The net income of $7,500 is *much more* than the gross income of $1,500 of the first example above! No sacrifice is required to pay the tithe for the rich; only saying no to more luxuries. Tithing is so much easier for him not only because he makes more money, but because he pays much less tithe, relatively speaking. Out of a *net increase of $6,200 more* (7500-1300), he only tithes *$850 more* (1000-150) than the poor!

6

The point is, that the more one earns the easier it is to pay the tithe and it requires no sacrifice. What makes this scenario even more dismal for the poor person is when blessings are pronounced on tithers and curses pronounced on non-tithers, as applied in many sermons from Malachi 3:8-10. To people with much income tithing is good news. Easily meeting their obligation to God, plus the additional promised blessings for tithing makes tithing a win-win situation. The poor does not only feel the stress of poverty but lives in fear of a curse coming upon her if she doesn't pay her tithe. Either she tries to sacrifice to pay it – after all, "it belongs to God" – or does not pay it and lives not only under fear, but, potentially, under guilt and condemnation. On the other hand, the rich may be lulled into false security thinking they have fulfilled their obligation to God.

If we think there is something wrong with this scenario, we should ask the question: "Is this what God intended when He instituted the tithe?" Could have, perhaps, the biblical tithe been misunderstood, misinterpreted and, thereby, misapplied today? Are we interpreting the tithe correctly? These very important and pertinent questions today should find a clear answer in this book.

While many teachers dogmatically hold onto the tithe as ten percent of income, there are others who do not. In fact, a silent controversy is brewing over what this term actually means and represents. What are the other viewpoints? Let us explore.

Exploring the Meaning/Definition of Tithing Today

"Your guess is as good as mine!" – could describe the way many view tithing today. Tithing is a term very commonly used by both pastors and laymen. One might expect it to mean the same to everyone, from its common usage, but that is not so. A close ear to what is preached and to what people say they believe reveals a broad spectrum of opinions and interpretations.

At first, mentioning the tithe conjures up one of two main responses. One is that tithing is an Old Testament concept which came and went with the Mosaic Law, and it does not apply to us today. The other, which is a set of responses, use the term "tithe" to describe some form of giving. Many in this category view tithing as an important biblical concept that is both applicable today and is wise to heed.

Once the term "tithing" is used in one's vocabulary, its definition ranges far and wide. Most people define the tithe as ten percent of income. However, when it comes to being more specific, that is, whether it should be of the gross, net, or of all sources of income including gifts, etc., one finds no agreement. I have heard arguments for all. But not even everyone agrees on the ten percent. Some pastors and ministry leaders call any amount they receive a "tithe" by virtue of it being "given to God." Thus, "tithing" is a term used loosely and is interchangeable with "giving."

As to how and where the tithe should be paid, the most common understanding is that the tithe belongs to one's local church where regular giving helps under-gird her many ministry expenses. Others teach a simple application: the tithe belongs where one is spiritually fed. Naturally this may be the local church, but it may be a para-church ministry that teaches the Word. Others see the tithe's purpose as meeting needs. Thus, the tithe may be given to support missionaries, charitable organizations, or to help the poor. Some save up their tithes and wait till the Holy Spirit tells them to where or to whom to give it. As for a unique interpretation, one lady confided in me that she gives her tithe to her daughter and husband who need help providing for their children. One is led to conclude that tithing means different things to different people.

A recently taken poll by Lifeway Research confirms the above observations. One thousand and ten Americans who attend services at a Protestant or nondenominational church at least once a month, and

1,000 Protestant senior pastors were asked their opinions on a wide variety of topics pertaining to tithing: from how they define the tithe, to where they tithe, to whether they think it is biblical to tithe, etc. Here are some of their conclusions:

> Seventy-two percent of pastors say tithing is "a biblical command that still applies today." Twenty-five percent say it is not. Three percent are not sure. Of pastors who say tithing is still a biblical command, 73 percent define tithing as giving 10 percent of a person's income. More than half (56 percent) say it should be 10 percent of a person's gross income. Seventeen percent say it should be 10 percent of a person's net income. Eleven percent say a tithe is whatever a person sets aside to give, while 7 percent say it is whatever the person actually gives.

The most astounding conclusions of the poll was that "Pastors are less likely than churchgoers to say tithing is still a biblical command." Why that would be the case is an interesting question, but it is not unreasonable to attribute the reason to one's understanding of the term "tithe." Tithing and giving are interchangeable terms in many people's minds as is indicated in the following poll observation:

> Most churchgoers say the Bible commands them to give. But their tithes don't always go in the offering plate. Half of Protestant churchgoers say their tithes can go to a Christian ministry rather than a church. A third say tithes can go to help an individual in need. And more than a few (18 percent) say tithes can even go to a secular charity, according to a new study by Nashville-based Lifeway Research. "For many churchgoers, tithing is just another term for generosity," said Scott McConnell, executive director of Lifeway Research. (https://lifewayresearch.com/2018/05/10 /churchgoers-say-they-tithe-but-not-always-to-the-church/)

Seeing the inconclusiveness and confusion over tithing, one can't help but ask the question, "Does the Bible not offer instructions on tithing that we need to come up with our own interpretations? Why is there

9

such confusion? The word "tithe" has been used to denote many things, but we, at large, typically are not aware of that fact. It can represent meanings as different as "apples" and "oranges," which are incomparable. "Apples" could refer to the many "varieties" of interpretations today, and "oranges" to the Bible's definition. While we might be aware of some of the ways the tithe is interpreted today, likely most of us do not know how the Bible defines the tithe. Is it not time to find out?

Tithing is a topic that can only be understood in context of the whole counsel of God on tithing. Every verse relates to another in some way. The most often taught passage on tithing is Malachi 3:8-10. What is the context of Malachi 3:8-10? The meaning and context of this passage cannot be understood outside the context of the Mosaic Law. The definition of the tithe referred to in this passage is important to understand, but this passage says nothing about it – that was established long before the writing of Malachi, and which the recipients of the book were well familiar with.

Common questions about tithing are: "Why did Abraham tithe? What was Jacob's vow all about? Why does the New Testament mention tithing?" All these questions cannot be fully answered without a detailed, comprehensive study of the tithe in the Bible. This undertaking is not as formidable as it might sound. I had frequently heard it said that "tithing is throughout the Bible." Therefore, I was quite shocked when I learned that the total number of references to the tithe come to 17 verses/passages! The statement that "tithing is throughout the Bible" might be according to one's own interpretation of what they understand tithing to mean. PART I of this book is an exposition of the biblical tithe – an exploration of all tithing passages in their scriptural contexts.

PART II explores the concept of giving. To give is a mandate and a very important principle in God's Word. The essence of God is "wrapped up" in loving and giving, and, having been made in His image and born into His family, we have inherited this nature from God. We are (to be) givers. What should we give? How much? To whom? When? Where? How? Why? Key New Testament Scriptures are examined to find the answers.

The reason for giving has gained much emphasis and attention in prosperity teachings. Tithing and giving are foundational to this gospel particularly because they bring financial harvest to the individual. PART III seeks answers from the Bible to questions such as: What is prosperity? How does the Bible define it? How does one attain it? Do giving and prosperity correlate? A discussion on wealth and riches in God's Word will also be included in this section.

This book, in essence, is a response to a prosperity teaching I heard over the course of many years. It follows then that familiarity with it is helpful. Here is a synopsis:

Prosperity Doctrine

The prosperity doctrine is founded on the belief that it is God's will for every Christian to prosper – namely to be rich and wealthy – and that the way to attain prosperity is through giving. The premise begins with the fact that Christ is the Seed of Abraham. It is believed, therefore, that in Him – in Christ – believers have inherited Abraham's blessings, namely, his wealth and riches (Genesis 12:2-3; Galatians 3:13-14). These riches, however, are stored up in heaven and can only be accessed through giving. Ephesians 1:3 is the basis for this understanding: "Blessed be the God and Father of our Lord Jesus Christ, who has blessed us with every spiritual blessing in the heavenly places in Christ." "Spiritual blessings" in this Scripture is taken to include riches on earth.

Giving, the teaching continues, can only begin after one's tithes are paid, for the tithe belongs to God (Leviticus 27:30, Malachi 3:8-10).

11

The tithe is defined as ten percent of one's gross income and should be paid to one's local church. Paying the tithe causes God to open the windows of heaven to pour out many blessings, however not paying the tithe causes the removal of God's protection over one's life, leaving the door open to curses (Malachi 3:8-10).

Giving into the kingdom is compared to a farmer sowing his seed to reap a harvest. The seed represents money, and the soil represents the place, person, or ministry the money is sown into. Sowing is considered an investment in a heavenly bank account where nothing can destroy and where the money earns dividends. What dividends one earns on his investment depends on the type of soil he sows into, for not all soil is the same.

According to this doctrine, the best soils to sow into are the church, the pastors (those over us in the Lord), and the "blessed," namely, rich Christians. Why the rich? This is also derived from Abraham's blessing. Abraham was very blessed and very rich, and God said: "I will bless them that bless thee" (Genesis 12:2-3). Since wealth comes as a result of God's blessing, sowing into the "blessed," or the rich, is one way to get the best return on one's sowing. The key is to sow "upward." Great financial harvests of 30-60-100-fold is promised to those who thus sow. However, the least profitable ground to sow into is the poor, for investing into them earns no interest at all. One only gets back what they sowed: "He who has pity on the poor lends to the Lord, And He will pay back what he has given" (Proverbs 19:17). The farmer's goal is not seed in the ground, the teaching goes, but the harvest, thus it is in the farmer's interest to sow promptly so it can begin to work for them.

What is taught by this doctrine is that the act of giving, to which tithing is foundational, has an intrinsic power to draw on the blessings of God (riches). Galatians 6:7 is used to prove this principle: "Be not deceived; God is not mocked: for whatsoever a man sows, that shall he also reap." From this verse it has also been preached that it is not so much where one sows but sowing alone will bring in a financial harvest. The power is in the sowing.

This is the summary of the doctrine in a nutshell. As some confusion has risen about tithing and giving – with some people tithing out of fear or obligation, while others out of expectation of an exorbitant harvest for self – a fresh look at the Scriptures in their contexts is critical. Giving should be an act of worship. What pleases God is giving freely, cheerfully, out of conviction and by the prompting of the Holy Spirit. He told us to be generous. He told us to take care of each other – particularly of the orphans and the widows – and to consider other people more important than ourselves (Philippians 2:3 Amp.).

The heart of this book is to help us recognize if we have misunderstood the Scriptures and followed a course that leads away from the Word and into bondage or self-interest. I pray His grace will reveal the truth. Jesus said, "You shall know the truth, and the truth shall set you free" (John 8:32). Only the truth that we know can set us free to be who we were created to be. May this book be a conduit for that pursuit!

PART I: TITHING

THE BIBLICAL TITHE: SCRIPTURAL OVERVIEW

The summary of all verses or passages that mention the tithe, in order of appearance, is as follows:

Old Testament:
Abraham's tithe: Genesis 14:20
Jacob's vow: Genesis 28:22
Mosaic tithe: Leviticus 27:30-32
                         Numbers 18:20-28
                         Deuteronomy 12:5-19; 14:22-29; 26:12-14
                         2 Chronicles 31:4-12
                         Nehemiah 10:37-39; 12:44; 13:5,12
                         Malachi 3:7-11

New Testament:
References to the Mosaic (Levitical) tithe: Matthew 23:23; Luke 11:42, 18:12
Reference to the Mosaic (Levitical) and Abrahamic tithes: Hebrews 7:1-9

This list reveals much important information: (1) Tithing appears predominantly in the Old Testament. (2) The New Testament Scriptures merely refer to the Old Testament tithes. (3) Besides Abraham's tithe and Jacob's vow, all the passages pertain to the Mosaic Law. (4) There is no reference to any other type of tithing in the Bible.

Since tithing is predominantly in the Law, the study will begin with the Mosaic tithe, which will be followed by Abraham's tithe, Jacob's vow, and the New Testament Scriptures on tithing.

TITHING: OLD TESTAMENT
Mosaic Tithe

As a precursor to this in-depth study, a quick attention needs to be given to the importance of studying the Bible in context. Context is the first rule of proper Bible exegesis. Both immediate and larger contexts are vitally important. The larger context – into which the tithe was birthed – begins the story. When was it birthed? It was birthed right after the fall of man into sin. The story unfolds a deep, deep love of a Creator for His creation – mankind. As strange as it may sound, tithing is imbedded in a beautiful love story.

God's Love

Tithing is most often thought of as one of God's ordinances described in the Mosaic laws. While that is true, it is important to recognize that it is not just one of many, many ordinances. Behind every action of God and every action He ordained men to observe is His infinite love. Every ordinance is designed to ensure the fulfillment of the two greatest commandments: "Love the Lord thy God with all your heart, soul and mind," and "love thy neighbor as thyself" (Matthew 22:37-40). God's heart towards us is that we learn to fear Him and to love each other. Every thread in the Old and New Testaments points us to and teaches us about His infinite love so that we might be like Him.

God's Plan of Redemption

In the Genesis account we learn about Adam and Eve disobeying God, which put them under a curse. Besides the curses God pronounced on Adam, Eve, and the ground, they lost intimate fellowship with their Creator. This could have been their end, if God, in His infinite grace, mercy, loving-kindness and wisdom, did not have a plan that gave man another chance to relate to Him and to receive His protection and blessings.

God had a long and elaborate plan. It would eventually result in complete restoration of men to Himself through His Son, Jesus Christ. But at first, God set out to teach a nation, through many laws, precepts, and ordinances, that loving Him and one another meant obedience. Learning to follow and obey all His commandments would also ensure God's presence, His blessings, and freedom from the curse. A holy nation was birthed from Abraham's descendants and through his promised child Isaac. Through this lineage would eventually be born the Savior of the world, Messiah, God's Son, Jesus. This choice nation, Israel, was *formed* into a nation in the desert of Sinai after their miraculous deliverance from Egypt.

Holy Nation, Holy Living

The first time the word "holy" appears in the Bible is in Exodus 3:5. It signified the time God came down to earth to begin the process of separating out for Himself a nation for the fulfillment of His plan on earth. The angel of the Lord suddenly appeared to Moses, God's choice leader, and instructed him to take off his sandals, for he was standing on "holy" ground. Later, after their miraculous deliverance from Egypt, on Mt. Sinai, God made a covenant with his people. This covenant included the condition for His continuing Holy presence with them, which is consecrated, holy living:

> Exodus 19:5 Now therefore, if you will indeed obey My voice and keep My covenant, then you shall be a special treasure to Me above all people; for all the earth is Mine. 6 And you shall be to Me a kingdom of priests and a holy nation.

What does "holy" mean? The Hebrew word for holy is "*qodesh*," (*Strong's Exhaustive Concordance*, #6944) and it means, "a sacred place or thing; consecrated (thing), dedicated (thing), hallowed (thing)." So, when we read the phrase "holy unto the Lord," we read something is consecrated, dedicated, and set apart for God, and must, therefore, be strictly handled according to God's specifications.

Once in a covenant relationship, God had to establish His holy dwelling place and place of worship – the Tabernacle. The book of Exodus details the building of the Tabernacle and the preparation of the priests for service. The following book, Leviticus, presents all the detailed instructions for the priests and people to follow for holy living. Not surprisingly, the words "holy" or "holiness" appear over 100 times in the book of Exodus, and over 150 times in the book of Leviticus with the recurring theme "You shall be holy, for I am holy." What are holy things? The book of Leviticus begins with "most holy" offerings to the Lord such as the cereal, sin, and trespass offerings, and continues with numerous ordinances and precepts for holy living. Everything pertaining to their relationship with God was considered holy, and as such we read about: holy convocation, habitation, Sabbath, men, place, garment, atonement, animals, one's house, field, and the *tithe*. The book of Leviticus ends with defining the holy tithe:

> Leviticus 27:30 And all the tithe of the land, whether of the seed of the land or of the fruit of the tree, is the Lord's. It is holy to the Lord. 31 If a man wants at all to redeem any of his tithes, he shall add one-fifth to it. 32 And concerning the tithe of the herd or the flock, of whatever passes under the rod, the tenth one shall be holy to the Lord.

Definition of the Tithe:
Tenth of Increase of the Land and Flock

What is the tithe? The word "tithe" is most commonly understood to mean "tenth." Interestingly, there are several Hebrew words that mean "tenth" and are translated as such in our English Bibles, except "*mahasar*" (*Strong's,* #4643) and "*asar*" (*Strong's,* #6237) which are most often translated as "tithe," "tithes," or "tithing." (Depending on translator.) We find these words associated with the tithes of Moses and

Abraham and Jacob's vow. One is curious as to why these Hebrew words are translated as "tithe" and not as "tenth."

A distinction seems to be evident in Leviticus 27:30-32. *Mahasar* is the Hebrew word used for the tithe. If *mahasar* had simply meant tenth, "tithe of the land" would imply tenth of the physical land. But the passage clarifies the tithe to be "... of the seed of the land, or of the fruit of the tree," namely, of the produce of the land. Also, the tithe (*mahasar)* is "of the herd or the flock." Since the Bible uses the term "increase" for the produce of the land and the multiplication of the herd and the flock (see Deut. 14:22, 26:12, 28:4,11, etc.), the tithe could be named: "tenth of increase of the land, herd and flock," or for short, "tenth of increase." I believe this is significant, because from this increase is what the tithe is paid on a perpetual basis.

Increase Comes by the Hand of God

For there to be increase of the land and livestock, the tribes had to get established in the land promised to them in the Abrahamic Covenant (Genesis 12:1,7; 13:14-17; 15). The land was their inheritance, free for the taking – a gift. Their part was only to move in and possess it with the Lord's help of driving out the nations before them (Joshua 23:5, Deuteronomy 6:18-19). They received with the land even more than what they could imagine. They received cities, houses, vineyards, and all kinds of good things – everything the land contained:

> Deuteronomy 6:10 So it shall be, when the Lord your God brings you into the land of which He swore to your fathers, to Abraham, Isaac, and Jacob, to give you large and beautiful cities which you did not build, 11 houses full of all good things, which you did not fill, hewn-out wells which you did not dig, vineyards and olive trees which you did not plant...

The tribes enjoyed instant capital and ownership of all things, including animals. Increase was the outcome as the land produced the harvest and flocks multiplied by the hand and blessing of God:

> Leviticus 26:3 If you walk in My statutes and keep My commandments, and perform them, 4 then I will give you rain in its season, the land shall yield its produce, and the trees of the field shall yield their fruit. 5 Your threshing shall last till the time of vintage, and the vintage shall last till the time of sowing; you shall eat your bread to the full, and dwell in your land safely.

From this increase the tribes were required to pay their tithes. The tithe – tenth – was the same portion required from all tribes. For it to be fair and equitable a fair distribution of land was necessary. This is exactly what happened as we read in the following account.

Before entering the Promised land God instructed Moses to: "Take a census of the whole Israelite community by families—all those twenty years old or more who are able to serve in the army of Israel." (Numbers 26:2, NIV) The reason for this count God explained this way:

> Numbers 26:53 "The land is to be allotted to them as an inheritance based on the number of names. 54 To a larger group give a larger inheritance, and to a smaller group a smaller one; each is to receive its inheritance according to the number of those listed. 55 Be sure that the land is distributed by lot. What each group inherits will be according to the names for its ancestral tribe. (NIV)

The fact that the larger tribes got larger inheritances and smaller tribes got smaller ones indicates that the land was divided fairly among families. This original divine allotment was to be kept for generations to come. A fair and equitable distribution of land ensured an equitable contribution of the tithes.

"...all the tithe of the land, whether of the seed of the land, or of the fruit of the tree, is the LORD's: it is holy unto the LORD." (27:30); "And ... the tithe of the herd, or of the flock... the tenth *shall be holy unto the LORD.*" (27:32)

The tithe was holy as it had a special purpose pertaining to man's relationship with God. Tithing was to be a continual observance – a practice of giving out of continual increase by the hand of God: "Then I will give you rain in due season, and the land shall yield her increase, and the trees of the field shall yield their fruit." (Lev. 26:4) Being holy, tithing had to follow very clear and intricate instructions such as: what to tithe on, for what purpose, to whom, how much, where, when, how, and how often. As to what to tithe on, it has already been established - - it was on the increase of the land and livestock. Consequently, the tithe was *food.* Who did the tithe (food) belong to and why? The answers to these questions turn out to be quite elaborate. God did not institute one, but two different tithes with three different recipients.

Recipients of the Tithe
The first tithe: Levitical Tithe
Numbers 18:20-32

The next mention of the tithe in the Bible is in Numbers 18:20-32. This passage teaches us about the Levitical tithe. Who were the Levites?

The Levites were one of the original twelve tribes of Israel, whom God chose to separate out as holy to Himself: "Now behold, I Myself have taken the Levites from among the children of Israel instead of every firstborn who opens the womb among the children of Israel. Therefore the Levites shall be Mine." (Numbers 3:3) The exact exchange is described in Numbers chapter three. To keep the tribes' count at twelve after the Levites' separation, Joseph's two sons each became a tribe. (Joseph was one of the twelve sons of Israel.)

21

The Levitical tribe had a special calling to serve in the Tabernacle. The Tabernacle was God's dwelling place on earth among His people. God required holy sacrifices and offerings to be brought to Him regularly from the people for the atoning of their sins, and these had to be offered and administered in a very specific way which required the ministry of the Priests and Levites of the Levitical tribe.

> Numbers 8:19 And I have given the Levites as a gift to Aaron and to his sons from among the children of Israel, to do the service of the children of Israel in the Tabernacle of the congregation, and to make an atonement for the children of Israel: that there be no plague among the children of Israel, when the children of Israel come nigh unto the sanctuary.

As to how to meet this consecrated tribe's needs, God had a unique plan. Instead of being given an equal portion of land as their inheritance, which the rest of the tribes received when the Promised land was distributed among the families, the Levites were assigned the *tithes* in Israel as their inheritance (besides a few cities they inherited):

> Numbers 18:20 Then the LORD said to Aaron: "You shall have no inheritance in their land, nor shall you have any portion among them; I am your portion and your inheritance among the children of Israel. 18:21 Behold, I have given the children of Levi all the tithes in Israel as an inheritance in return for the work which they perform, the work of the tabernacle of meeting.

To the Priest God said, "I am your portion and your inheritance among the children of Israel." To the Levites God said, "I have given the children of Levi all the tithes in Israel as an inheritance." So, while all the *land* was given to all the twelve tribes, one tenth *of the increase* of the land was withheld from them and was assigned to the Levites for *their* inheritance. So, paying the tithes was the same as giving them to the rightful owners. It follows then, that paying the tithes was not only an act of obedience to God, but it was also a payment for the Levites' services in the Tabernacle (v.21). To withhold the tithe was a very serious offence, not only because it meant stealing someone else's goods, but because it was their literal food supply. This is why the charge is so serious in Malachi 3:8-11, the most often quoted and familiar passage on tithing today.

The tithes were directly related to offerings. As the people brought their animals to be sacrificed for their burnt, sin, peace, or guilt/trespass offerings, the Levites were indispensable to the Priests in preparing and presenting those offerings to the Lord according to His many specifications. The distinction between tithes and offerings was that the offerings were brought by the people *to God* for the continuous atonement for their sins, while the tithes were brought *to the Levites* (men) as their perpetual inheritance for their work in the tabernacle.

The Priests and Levites' dependence on the people to bring their offerings and to pay their tithes brings to light God's design for His kingdom: men's mutual dependence on one another. Everyone, including the Priests and Levites, was dependent on the priesthood for the forgiveness of their sins. The Priests and Levites were dependent on their "brothers'" integrity and obedience to bring in their tithes to survive. (Unfortunately, each were given a free will and many of them failed to fulfill their obligations.)

The Second Tithe
Deuteronomy 12:1-19; 14:22-29; and 26:12-14

"Deuteronomy" means "second lawgiving." Standing on the East side of the Jordan River, the tribes were about to enter and conquer their inheritance - the Promised Land. Moses, who was not allowed to enter the Promised Land, reminded the people of God's love-covenant. He encouraged them to never forget their God but to obey Him continually. It will go well with them if they follow the Lord and His commandments, but they will encounter great sufferings and curses if

23

they do not. Amid these instructions the tithe is mentioned, but in some new light.

A second tithe is introduced which is divided up in a six-year Sabbatical cycle. It is designed to serve two different purposes. In years 1, 2, 4 and 5 of the six-year cycle the owner is instructed to eat his tithe. In the third and sixth years the owner is to give his tithe to the poor and the Levites. Here were the instructions:

Second tithe: A. **_Eaten by the owner_**. Deuteronomy 12:1-19, 14:22-27.

> Deuteronomy 12:1 These are the statutes and judgments which you shall be careful to observe in the land which the LORD God of your fathers is giving you to possess, all the days that you live on the earth.... 12:5 ... you shall seek the place where the LORD your God chooses, out of all your tribes, to put His name for His dwelling place; and there you shall go. 12:6 There [where His Name dwells - Jerusalem] you shall take your burnt offerings, your sacrifices, your _tithes_, the heave offerings of your hand, your vowed offerings, your freewill offerings, and the firstborn of your herds and flocks. 12:7 And there _you shall eat_ before the LORD your God, and _you shall rejoice_ in all to which you have put your hand, you and your households, in which the LORD your God has blessed you... 12:12 And _you shall rejoice_ before the LORD your God, you and your sons and your daughters, your male and female servants, and the Levite who is within your gates, since he has no portion nor inheritance with you. (Emphasis added)

Here is another tenth of the produce of the land (of what remains after the first tenth has been given to the Levites) which the owner now was directed to eat with great rejoicing and celebration! Being "holy," this tithe, along with the other offerings, has specific instructions to follow. For one, it had to be taken to where God dwelt (Jerusalem) and eaten there. It could not be eaten in any other place, including one's own town. This is emphasized once again in verse 17:

24

Deuteronomy 12:17 You may *not eat within your gates* the tithe of your grain or your new wine or your oil, of the firstborn of your herd or your flock, of any of your offerings which you vow, of your freewill offerings, or of the heave offering of your hand. 12:18 But *you must eat them before the LORD your God in the place which the LORD your God chooses,* you and your son and your daughter, your male servant and your female servant, and the Levite who *is* within your gates; and you shall rejoice before the LORD your God in all to which you put your hands. 12:19 Take heed to yourself that you do not forsake the Levite as long as you live in your land. (Emphasis added)

It is worthy to notice that God reminded the people every time to not forget the Levites. The next passage points out God's concern about his children being over-burdened on their way to the celebration and offers a solution. While one of the purposes of this trip was to teach them to fear the Lord always (v. 23), He loves and cares for His people whom He desires to lavish with abundant joy and happiness.

Deuteronomy 14:22 You shall truly *tithe* all the increase of your grain that the field produces year by year. 23 And you shall *eat* before the Lord your God, in the place where He chooses to make His name abide, the tithe of your grain and your new wine and your oil, of the firstborn of your herds and your flocks, *that you may learn to fear the Lord your God always.*

24 But if the journey is too long for you, so that you are not able to carry the tithe, or if the place where the Lord your God chooses to put His name is too far from you, when the Lord your God has blessed you, 25 then you shall exchange it for money, take the money in your hand, and go to the place which the Lord your God chooses. 26 And you shall spend that money for whatever your heart desires: for oxen or sheep, for wine or similar drink, for whatever your heart desires; you shall eat there before the Lord your God, and you shall rejoice, you and your

household. 27 You shall not forsake the Levite who is within your gates, for he has no part nor inheritance with you. (NKJV) (emphasis added)

God literally mandated men to enjoy the fruits of their labor while remembering Him, His provisions, and blessings. The celebration was at God's bidding at His designated place and time, and with Him in focus on His goodness and love for mankind.

The Israelites were to observe this ordinance for two years, and in the third year God had a different plan. Instead of eating the tithe themselves with their household and the Levites, they were to give it to the Levites and the poor in one's town:

*Second tithe: B. **Given to the poor.*** Deuteronomy 14:28-29, 26:12-14.

> The above passage continues:
> 28 "At the end of every third year you shall bring out *the tithe* of your produce of that year and store it up within your gates. 29 And the *Levite,* because he has no portion nor inheritance with you, *and the stranger and the fatherless and the widow who are within your gates,* may come and eat and be satisfied, that the Lord your God may bless you in all the work of your hand which you do. (Emphasis added)

"Gates" refers to towns. In other words, the tithe was to be brought to a place in one's own town from which the Levites, the strangers, the orphans and the widows would get their share. To ensure that they had followed all His specific instructions pertaining to the poor tithe, God led the people in the following confession:

> Deuteronomy 26:12 "When you have finished laying aside all the tithe of your increase in the third year—the year of tithing—and have given it to the Levite, the stranger, the fatherless, and the widow, so that they may eat within your gates and be filled, 13 then you shall say before the Lord your God: 'I have removed the holy tithe from my house, and also have given them to the Levite, the stranger, the

fatherless, and the widow, according to all Your commandments which You have commanded me; I have not transgressed Your commandments, nor have I forgotten them. 14 I have not eaten any of it when in mourning, nor have I removed any of it for an unclean use, nor given any of it for the dead. I have obeyed the voice of the Lord my God, and have done according to all that You have commanded me. (NKJV)

To summarize the ordinances for all the tithes I conclude with this quote from the New Standard Jewish Encyclopedia:

> "The Jewish law lists various obligatory tithes. (1) The Levitical tithe (Nu.18:24),
> (2) Second tithe (Lev. 27:31; Deut. 14:22-26), i.e., an additional tenth taken after the first tithe. This was eaten by the owner himself in Jerusalem. It applied only during the 1st, 2nd, 4th and 5th years of the Sabbatical cycle, (3) the Poor tithe (Deut. 14:28-29; 26:12), given to the poor and replacing the second tithe in the 3rd and 6th year of the Sabbatical cycle. (4) Tithe of the animals (Lev. 17:32) selected in the thrice yearly counting and offered as a sacrifice by the owner."
> (Edited by Dr. Geoffrey Wigoder D. Phil., Fifth Edition, Doubleday & Company Inc., Garden City, New York, 1977 pp 1862-1863).

Much has been already covered about the biblical tithe. Each book of the Bible that mentioned the tithe so far offered new information about it. What will the remainder of the books – 2 Chronicles, Nehemiah and Malachi – teach? Thinking in terms of today's concept of tithing – of regularly giving ten percent of our income to God weekly, biweekly, or monthly – overlooks a problem the tribes had to face. The tithe was food, not money, which was to be taken to Jerusalem once a year when the harvest came in. God dwelt and the Priests and Levites worked in the Temple in Jerusalem. Thus, the Levitical tithes needed to be stored somewhere. This is exactly the topic the next books of the Bible cover.

Storing the Tithe
2 Chronicles 31:4-12; Nehemiah 10:37-39; 12:44; 13:5,12;
Malachi 3:7-11

Both, King Hezekiah and Nehemiah, worked on restoring the temple, temple worship, and service to the Lord in their days. As the processes are described, one gets a glimpse into how the tithes were collected and stored.

Tithes were received in the temple once a year from the third month to the seventh month (2 Chronicles 31:7). As the harvest was coming in, the accumulated products required a storage place. As part of the restoration of the temple and worship, King Hezekiah ordered the people living in Jerusalem to give the portion due to the Priests and Levites. Then, he made plans to store what came in (2 Chronicles 31:4-12):

> 31:5... the children of Israel brought in abundance the firstfruits of corn, wine, and oil, and honey, and of all the increase of the field; and the *tithe of all things* brought they in abundantly. 31:6 ... they also brought in *the tithe of oxen and sheep*, and *the tithe of holy things* which were consecrated unto the LORD their God, and laid them by heaps... 31:11 Then Hezekiah commanded to prepare *chambers* in the house of the LORD; and they prepared them.

Nehemiah commanded the Levites also to bring their tithes (from the tithes they received), to be given to the Priests, which will be stored in chambers. Nehemiah 10:38-39:

> "...and the Levites shall bring up the tithe of the tithes *unto the house of our God, to the chambers*, into the treasure house. For the children of Israel and the children of Levi shall bring the offering of the corn, of the new wine, and the oil, *unto the chambers* ... and we will not forsake the house of our God."

"Not forsaking the house of God" meant bringing in the tithes and offerings. Understanding how the tithes and offerings were stored and that they were the Priests' and Levites' food supply, makes the last and most often quoted passage on tithing in the Old Testament more easily understood. God so addressed the sons of Jacob in Malachi 3:7-11:

> Malachi 3:7 Even from the days of your fathers ye are gone away from mine ordinances, and have not kept them. Return unto me, and I will return unto you, saith the LORD of hosts. But ye said, Wherein shall we return? 8 Will a man rob God? Yet ye have robbed me. But ye say, Wherein have we robbed thee? In tithes and offerings. 9 Ye are cursed with a curse: for ye have robbed me, even this whole nation. 10 Bring ye all the tithes into the storehouse, that there may be meat in mine house, and prove me now herewith, saith the LORD of hosts, if I will not open you the windows of heaven, and pour you out a blessing, that there shall not be room enough to receive it. 11 And I will rebuke the devourer for your sakes, and he shall not destroy the fruits of your ground; neither shall your vine cast her fruit before the time in the field, saith the LORD of hosts.

Read in today's context, this passage makes absolutely no sense. In the context of the Mosaic Law and temple worship this passage is very easily understood. The tithe was food, given to the Levites, who in turn tithed to the Priests. This food was stored in storehouses (chambers) in the temple. Without the tithes and offerings, the Priests and Levites had no provision. Without provision they could not fulfill their priestly duties as mediators between God and men. Separation from God meant removal of God's protection and blessings. Men were back under the curse.

The Message of Malachi

Bringing the tithes and offerings into the storehouse represented obedience to God. Obedience brought the blessings of God on the land:

> Leviticus 26:3 If ye walk in my statutes, and keep my commandments, and do them; 4 Then I will give you rain

in due season, and the land shall yield her increase, and the trees of the field shall yield their fruit.

5 And your threshing shall reach unto the vintage, and the vintage shall reach unto the sowing time: and ye shall eat your bread to the full, and dwell in your land safely.

Disobeying God brought the curse back upon them:

> Leviticus 26:15 And if ye shall despise my statutes, or if your soul abhors my judgments, so that ye will not do all my commandments, but that ye break my covenant: 16 I also will do this unto you ... ye shall sow your seed in vain, for your enemies shall eat it.... 19 ... I will break the pride of your power; and I will make your heaven as iron, (yielding no answer, no blessing, no rain [Amp.]) and your earth as (sterile as [Amp.]) brass: 20 And your strength shall be spent in vain: for your land shall not yield her increase, neither shall the trees of the land yield their fruits.

The message is simply this: men were under the curse after the fall. God provided "a way of escape" through His ordinances and precepts. Obedience brought the "covering" of blessings upon them. These included protection from their enemies, abundant increase of the land and of all they possessed, protection from all kinds of sicknesses and diseases, and more. As long as they obeyed, things went well, and they were truly blessed. Disobedience removed the covering, and they were back under a curse.

This passage in Malachi may have been God's last plea to these wayward people to call them to repentance (a change of heart and to do right again). He knew that by refusing to tithe and to bring the offerings to His storehouses to feed the Priests and Levites, they had in fact rejected Him. Without the mediators between God and men, the people had no chance to make anything right with God. Most importantly, receiving forgiveness and covering for their sins could only be obtained through sacrifices administered by the Levites. This is why He said, "Ye are cursed with a curse."

Should they have obeyed and restored the priestly office and temple worship, God would have opened the windows of Heaven. The rain and sunshine would have produced such a harvest, that there would have been no room enough to receive it. The covering of sins would have brought the release of blessings.

Unfortunately, that is not what happened. History tells that after this book was written God did not speak to men for 400 years. Not until Jesus came as a little baby that men could have relationship with God again, a relationship that surpassed anything men in the past could have ever imagined! What incredible mercy, love, and compassion!

Summary of the Mosaic Tithe

All (except for two) verses on tithing in the Old Testament have been carefully examined in context, and it has been established that all passages from Exodus to Malachi pertain to the Mosaic tithe instituted under the Mosaic Law.

Tithing could not begin until after two things were in place. One was the occupation of the Promised Land which God gave to the newly formed holy nation as their inheritance. The other was the consecration of the Levitical tribe. The Levites worked for God and the people to bring atonement for their sins. For their service, instead of land, the Levites inherited the tithe of the land and of livestock. Their portion of the land was given to the other tribes and each of the tribes pitched in (by giving tenth) to cover what the Levites' land would have produced. God made this a legal transaction by making the tithe of the land – namely, the tenth portion of the increase, or produce of the land – the Levites' rightful inheritance.

The nation, the Levites and the tithes were all holy and set apart for God. Thus, tithing was to be observed according to strict specifications. There was no room for guessing. God told the tribes specifically what to tithe on, to whom, where, when, how much, how often, in what manner, and for what purpose. The tithe was food to feed the Levites and the poor. They all had the means to give, as God gave them the land and blessed it. It would produce enough to meet one's needs, give the Levites their portion, and still have plenty to share. God did not ask for something the people did not have. The tithe was to be brought into the storehouse when the harvest first came in. The animals were brought to the Levites about three times a year.

In addition to the Levitical tithe, a second tithe was instituted for a different purpose. For two years of a Sabbatical cycle, it was to be taken to the Feasts in Jerusalem where the landowner was to eat his tithe in joyful celebration with his household and to share it with the Levites and the poor (the orphans, widows, and foreigners) who did not own land. In the third year of the Sabbatical cycle, he was to give his tithe to the Levites and the poor in his town. The cycle repeated, excluding the seventh year.

Obedient observance of the tithes and offerings enabled the Priests and Levites to fulfill their priestly services, which ensured God's manifest presence among them, the continuous forgiveness of their sins, and numerous other blessings of God upon their lives. The tribes, the Priests, and the Levites' mutual dependence on each other for their spiritual and physical survival reminded them of their continuous dependence on God's forgiveness of their sins. The Priest's service was a foreshadowing of the work of our final, perfect, eternal High Priest – Jesus Christ, the only true Mediator between God and men. Christ also became the final, perfect, and only acceptable sacrifice for the forgiveness of men's sins.

The specifics of the biblical tithe can be summarized as follows:

(1) Who is to tithe?   - the 12 tribes of Israel
(2) To whom?   - the Levites, the owner, widows, orphans, and strangers in the land

(3) Of what?	- the produce of the land and of the animals -- it was food
(4) For what purpose?	- to pay the Levites their inheritance, feed the poor, owner to attend feast
(5) How much?	- one tenth for the Levites, plus one tenth for the second tithe
(6) How often?	- once a year as the harvest came in
(7) Where?	- for the Levites and owner's feast: Jerusalem; for the poor: one's own town
(8) How?	- each tithe had its own specific guideline to follow: obediently, faithfully
(9) Was it obligatory?	- yes, the Mosaic tithe was obligatory

Is the Mosaic Law Applicable to Us Today?

Is tithing under the Law applicable today in any way? To answer this question, it is important to reiterate the meaning of the biblical tithe. A portion, such as tenth, is meaningless by itself and requires context – what it is tenth of, what is its purpose, how to apply it, etc. The Mosaic tithe was intricately defined in its meaning, purpose, and application.

Understanding this concept is at the very core and center of this book. The tithe we thought we understood – as taught and presented today -- and the tithe the Bible talks about are two different things. From Leviticus to Malachi the tithe had a very special and specific meaning which the Israelites understood throughout the ages, even to Jesus' day. The ordinance, definition and purpose had not changed. The tithe referred to in Malachi is the same as is in the book of Leviticus. The tithe was holy in all its attributes and to change any part of it is to misrepresent God's ordinance and His Word.

Thus, from a very practical standpoint, the Mosaic tithe cannot apply to us today. We do not have either the temple where animal sacrifices are offered regularly, or Levites to serve in the temple, who would receive the tithes. The tithe eaten by the owner was also taken to the

Feasts and was to be enjoyed following specific guidelines. To do it differently would be disobeying God. The Mosaic tithe cannot apply to us because it was not given to us. We are not under the system of law that God established for the children of Israel who were set apart for a very special relationship with God, and with whom God made His first Covenant. We are under a new Covenant that replaced the first, established by Jesus, the Son of God, who offered Himself as a final and perfect sacrifice to be shed for our sins:

> "In burnt offerings and sin offerings You have taken no delight. Then I said, Behold, here I am, coming to do Your will, O God - [to fulfill] what is written of Me in the volume of the Book. When He said just before, You have neither desired, nor have You taken delight in sacrifices and burnt offerings and sin offerings - all of which are offered according to the Law - He then went on to say, Behold, [here] I am, coming to do Your will. Thus He does away with and annuls the first (former) order [as a means of expiating sin] so that He might inaugurate and establish the second (latter) order. (Hebrew 10:6-9 Amp.)

Also,

> "When God speaks of a new [covenant or agreement], *He makes the first one obsolete (out of use)*. And what is obsolete (out of use and annulled because of age) is *ripe for disappearance and to be dispensed with altogether*" (Hebrew 8:13 Amp.) (Emphasis added)

As the Old Covenant passes, with it passes the Law and the instituted tithe. With Jesus everything changes – the Old Covenant becomes obsolete, and a New Covenant is ushered in. How the tithe is the key for Jewish readers to understand this transition will be discussed under the heading "Hebrews 7."

What Principles Can We Draw from the Mosaic Tithe?

Though the system of tithing described in the Mosaic Law does not apply to us, we can take away some very important principles. The tithe reveals much about God's heart and His plan for us. Every aspect of the Law is a shadow of things to come, and a reflection of God's relationship with us and with one another.

First, we learn that it is God's heart and intent is to provide for all of us. The tithe was all about food, and He instituted the tithe to make sure that those who had no land would have provision. Tithing so beautifully reflects God's two greatest commandments: to love Him with our whole heart, mind, and soul, and to love our neighbors as ourselves. As for the first, God developed an incredibly elaborate plan that would satisfy Him while He dwelt among sinful men here on earth. By approaching Him with their offerings, God would forgive the people's sins and would be pleased with them. God offered a way to seek and worship Him and made the invitation. He comes first and above all else. Obedience meant loving Him.

The second commandment is well exemplified in the second tithe. God provided a bountiful harvest for the landowner to enjoy and then directed him to share it with the Levites and the poor. By giving them the Law, God did not just give His children laws to follow, but by them guided them "in the way they should go," that is, in the way of loving their fellow men, and of being aware of the needy and sharing God's blessings with them. His system of tithing reflects His heart.

Secondly, and much related to this point, tithing represents a very interesting picture of sharing and inter-dependence between God and men and between men. With the tithe God positioned Himself to depend on the tribes' integrity and obedience to pay Him back what was His, while the tribes depended on God to provide rain and sunshine to bring in the harvest. In exchange for the tithe, the Levites served the tribes as mediators between God and them. The cycle exemplifies a beautiful, mutual inter-dependence and inter-connectedness between God, the Levites, and the tribes. God wants to be involved with us and wants us to be involved with one another. This is a very important principle we can take away from the tithe. While God does not need anything, He provides usually *through us*, and when we disobey and withhold what He prompts us to give to another, we end up robbing the other of a need or blessing God intended for them.

Thirdly, tithing points to the importance of obedience to God. Blessings overflow when we obey, and we worship Him when we obey. Tithing was not -- and was not meant to be -- sacrificial or burdensome. God did not want man's goods, the fruit of their labor, or their own sacrifices. He wanted to be worshiped and honored by *obeying His* plan. He gave them land and livestock, He increased and blessed each, and all He required from men was to return the portion He claimed for Himself. God repeatedly states in the Scriptures that He wants obedience and not sacrifice. Why was God unhappy in Malachi 3:8-10? Because by not obeying Him in bringing their proper offerings and tithes, they basically and ultimately rejected *Him* – His plans and His ways. Disobedience intercepted the flow between God and men, and between men and men. The sweetest sacrifice to Him is our obedience, which the most holy expression of worship.

With this ends the Mosaic Tithe. Attention now turns to Abraham's tithe and Jacob's vow. What is the significance of each?

Abrahamic Tithe
Genesis 14:16-20, Hebrews 7

Abraham's tithe falls into a different category from the Mosaic tithe. About 430 years before the Law was established, Abraham tithed (Galatians 3:17). We learn about it in Genesis 14:16-20 and Hebrews chapter 7, so we will study these passages together. The context of this tithe takes us back to the time when Abraham with his 318 trained servants had just miraculously won a great battle against four kings and their armies who had taken away his nephew Lot, his goods, and all the wealth of Sodom and Gomorrah (Gen. 14:11-12). After the victory, we read:

14:18 ... Melchizedek king of Salem brought forth bread and wine: and he was the priest of the most high God. 14:19 And he blessed him, and said, Blessed be Abram of the most high God, possessor of heaven and earth: 14:20 And blessed be the most high God, which hath delivered thine enemies into thy hand. And he gave him tithes of all.

To appreciate what happened here, five kings could not defeat four kings led by Chedorlaomer, yet Abraham defeated them with 318 trained servants! Not only did he slay Chedorlaomer and the kings who were with him, he also "brought back all the goods, and also brought again his brother Lot, and his goods, and the women also, and the people." (Genesis 14:16). When he returned from the battle, he had a very special encounter with a unique person and High Priest: Melchizedek. Over bread and wine this Priest of the Most High powerfully blessed Abraham. Abraham, in return, gave him tithes of all. Now, if tithing was not introduced till the Law was given much later by Moses, why did Abraham tithe?

The Bible does not specifically tell us why Abraham tithed, and we find no other record of him tithing in the Bible, even though he acquired great amount of wealth over the years. Considering what was different in this situation from any other time might give us a clue. The two main differences from other accounts are that (1) increase was on spoil of war miraculously won, and (2) a High Priest, who was also a King, showed up.

Could Abraham have tithed according to the custom of his day? The following quote from a secondary source has been used to suggest that idea:

"The practice of giving one tenth of the produce of the land and of the spoils of war to priests and kings was an ancient and deeply-rooted custom in existence for more than 400 years before the time of Moses and the giving of the Law." (Morris Cerullo's "Financial Breakthrough Spiritual Warfare Bible," (p. xxxiv.)

37

So, Abraham could have simply followed the custom of his day when he tithed, or could he? And could he have tithed more than once even though it has only been recorded once?

In the above quotation the kings and priests referred to are of other nations, as the nation of Israel was not born yet. The subjects tithed according to the custom of the day. The patriarchs, beginning with Abraham, from whom God eventually formed the nation Israel, did not belong to these nations. They had no kings over them, nor priests. We know that Noah, Abraham and the patriarchs brought offerings and burnt sacrifices to the Lord (Gen. 8:20, 22, 31:54, 46:1), but there is no mention of priests performing the duties. God considered them to be the priests. So, without kings and priests there was *no system* of tithing for the patriarchs. (Not until the priesthood was established by God for the nation Israel that the tithe was instituted, for the priesthood and tithing went hand in hand.)

Abraham could not have tithed, except to God, or to a High Priest of God, who would have been the only one above Abraham. The essence of Abraham's tithe rests in the identity of this person, Melchizedek.

Who was Melchizedek? Genesis already taught us that Melchizedek was King of Salem, the Priest of the Most High God, who brought forth bread and wine, and blessed Abram (Genesis 14:18). Hebrews chapter seven adds to this description:

> "For this Melchizedek, king of Salem [later called Jerusalem], priest of the most high God, who met Abraham returning from the slaughter of the kings, and blessed him; To whom also Abraham gave a tenth part of all; first being by interpretation **King of righteousness**, and after that also **King of Salem**, which is, **King of peace; Without father, without mother, without descent, having neither beginning of days, nor end of life; but made like unto the Son of God; abideth a priest continually**. (Hebrews 7:1-3). (Emphasis added)

Summarizing his attributes in the two passages we learn that he (was):

- King of Salem [later called Jerusalem]
- Priest of the Most High God
- King of righteousness
- King of peace
- brought forth bread and wine
- blessed Abram
- without father, without mother, without descent, having neither beginning of days, nor end of life
- made like unto the Son of God; abideth a priest continually.

He was undoubtedly greater than Abraham. The writer of the book of Hebrews, whom we will assume to be the Apostle Paul from now on, exclaims: "Now observe and consider how great (a personage) this was to whom even Abraham the patriarch gave a tenth (the topmost or the pick of the heap) of the spoil" (Hebrews 7:4 Amplified). "And without all contradiction the less is blessed of the better" (Hebrews 7:7). We know that Abraham was blessed by Melchizedek, and not vice versa. Further, Paul considers Melchizedek to be in the same order as Jesus, when he identifies Jesus as "a Priest forever after the order of Melchizedek" (Hebrews 5, 6, and 7).

If Melchizedek was a High Priest of God, with qualifications that belong to the Son of God, and was of the order of Jesus, he must have been Jesus, the pre-Incarnate Son of God Himself. He is believed to have appeared to men a few other times in the Old Testament, usually by the name "Angel of the Lord" (to Hagar in Genesis 16:7-11, to Abraham in Gen.22:11-12, to Jacob in Gen.31: 11,13, to Moses in Exodus 3:1-6, etc.). Could have Abraham, perhaps, recognized Him from his previous encounter?

Now, Abraham tithed on the spoil he just miraculously gained. The Hebrew word "*mahasar*," which is used here for "tithe," reflects the same meaning as discussed before: tenth of increase by God's hand, or in this case, by His supernatural provision. But this victory was not only about increase. It was about a miraculous deliverance and recovery of all things stolen. God sent the pre-Incarnate Jesus, the Priest of God Most High (the future Redeemer of mankind) to bring about deliverance and recovery for Abraham's nephew Lot. But not only for him, but the rest of the inhabitants of Sodom. Recognizing Melchizedek as such a High Priest, Abraham instinctively knew that he was to pay him tithes.

The custom of the day was to tithe to kings and priests. Melchizedek was both a King and a Priest, but in God's system it was the Priest who was appointed to receive the tithe. Abraham's tithe to this Priest was foundational in Paul's argument (in Hebrews chapter seven), that Jesus Christ became the new High Priest. Therefore, if tithes belong to the Priests, then for Abraham to tithe any other time, Melchizedek would have had to show up, for he was the only Priest he could have tithed to.

Now, it is worthy to note that while 90 percent of the spoil was his to keep, he gave it all to the king of Sodom, except the food his soldiers ate. He reasoned, "lest (he) should say 'I have made Abram rich.'" (Gen. 14:23)

Similarities Between the Levitical and Abrahamic Tithes

The Levitical and Abrahamic tithes were similar in two ways. First, Abraham tithed on what he miraculously gained by the hand of God. While some may argue that he himself fought, we cannot be so foolish as to believe that he defeated four kings and their armies with his 318 men! The Word says: "And blessed be the most high God, which hath delivered thine enemies into thy hand." (Genesis 14:20a). With the victory came the booty out of which "he gave him tithes of all." Abraham returned tenth of everything he gained to the High Priest. He did not run home to find some valuable offerings or money to bring to Melchizedek. He simply returned part of what he miraculously gained back. The second aspect is that he tithed to the Priest. In these two areas Abraham's tithe resembled the Levitical tithe.

Differences Between the Levitical and Abrahamic Tithes

While there were obvious similarities between the Levitical and Abrahamic tithes, there were also some stark differences between them. First, tithing under the Law was a continuous, obligatory observance. Tithing helped bring about the atonement for sins, and it literally fed the mediators between the people and God – the Levitical tribe. As for Abraham, he enjoyed a close, personal relationship with God and had no mediator -- he offered his own sacrifices and brought his own offerings to the Lord. We have a record of him only tithing once when the High Priest Melchizedek appeared to him, following victory over his enemies and recovery of things stolen.

Second, the tribes had to take their tithes to Jerusalem to the storehouse, while in the case of Abraham, Melchizedek the High Priest came to him.

Third, tithing *earned* God's favor and blessings under the Law. Tithing *preceded* the blessings and was necessary *to receive* the blessings. Not so with Abraham. He was blessed *first* and *then* he tithed: "And he (Melchizedek) blessed him, and said, Blessed be Abram of the most high God... And he (Abraham) gave him tithes of all." (Genesis 14:19-20).

Fourth, Abraham's tithe was a true return on the increase, while the Levitical tithe was paying the Levites their assigned inheritance. Only the handling of the tithe was given to the tribes, not ownership. Not tithing was literally stealing from the Levites.

The differences are sharp. Abraham's tithe was very different indeed and unique. Besides the fact that Abraham had an encounter with the

41

(Pre-Incarnate) Jesus and was blessed first before he tithed, we also see faith heavily exercised. To take on four formidable armies with 318 men, no matter how well trained they were, he must have had either a visitation or a word from God, or simply that much faith that God would show up on his behalf. Abraham's fight may not have been in the battle as much as in believing that God would rescue him. This faith must have profoundly pleased the Lord when He fought his battle for him and when He showed up with bread and wine.

The principle of Abraham's tithe reflects the grace principle of the New Testament. He exercised much faith and then it was God's miraculous, enabling power – grace – that saved him from the enemies' hands. Grace showed up not only in power but in a person of Melchizedek, who blessed Abraham. In line with the grace principle of the New Testament, Abraham was "saved (from his enemies) by 'Grace' (Jesus) through faith" (Ephesians 2:8), and *then* "gave him tithes of all."

If we just followed the Abrahamic tithe our preaching would be quite different. As he was blessed, he gave. Let us ask the following question: which order is the tithing teaching popular today patterned after – the Levitical tithe representing the Law, or the Abrahamic tithe before the Law? When tithing is preached out of Malachi with blessings and curses following tithing and not tithing, the answer is obvious: the Levitical tithe representing the Law. It is no wonder, as it is preached *from* the Law.

Abraham's tithe gives us much to ponder. What can we learn from Jacob's vow?

Jacob's Vow
Genesis 28:22

Jacob was on his way to his uncle Laban's place in Haran, fleeing from his brother Esau whose birthright he stole through trickery and deceit. Despite this questionable behavior, God was with Him fulfilling His promise to Abraham, and appeared to Jacob in a dream. In this dream he saw a ladder reaching heaven from earth and angels ascending and descending on it. We read:

> 13 And behold, the Lord stood above it and said: "I am the Lord God of Abraham your father and the God of Isaac; the land on which you lie I will give to you and your descendants. 14 Also your descendants shall be as the dust of the earth; you shall spread abroad to the west and the east, to the north and the south; and in you and in your seed all the families of the earth shall be blessed. 15 Behold, I am with you and will keep you wherever you go, and will bring you back to this land; for I will not leave you until I have done what I have spoken to you."

> 16 Then Jacob awoke from his sleep and said, "Surely the Lord is in this place, and I did not know it." 17 And he was afraid and said, "How awesome is this place! This is none other than the house of God, and this is the gate of heaven!"

> 18 Then Jacob rose early in the morning, and took the stone that he had put at his head, set it up as a pillar, and poured oil on top of it. 19 And he called the name of that place Bethel; but the name of that city had been Luz previously. 20 Then Jacob made a vow, saying, "If God will be with me, and keep me in this way that I am going, and give me bread to eat and clothing to put on, 21 so that I come back to my father's house in peace, then the Lord shall be my God. 22 And this stone which I have set as a pillar shall be God's house, and of all that You give me I will surely give a tenth to You." (Genesis 28:13-22)

What precipitated Jacob's vow in verse 22 was God's appearance to him in a dream. This was the Angel of the Lord (Genesis 31:11, 13) who assured Jacob of God's love, protection, and fulfillment of the promise He made to Abraham and his descendants. These sound too good to Jacob. As if to test everything the Angel said, he reiterated: " If God will be with me, and will keep me in this way that I go, and will give me bread to eat, and raiment to put on, So that I come again to my father's house in peace; then shall the Lord be my God: And this stone, which I have set for a pillar, shall be God's house: and of all that thou shalt give me I will surely give the tenth unto thee."

This vow to tithe was neither to be before nor after acquisition of wealth, but after the safe return to his father's house. His greatest fear was his brother, and his vow may have more to do with his protection, provision, and safety than anything else. His vow has a feel of testing or challenging God: "If... then shall the Lord be my God." Thus, the tenth may be a personal choice portion for his vow.

However, the tenth may have come about for two other reasons. One is having known about his grandfather Abraham tithing to the High Priest of God in a similar situation. The other is being influenced by the practice of ancient cultures, as mentioned earlier, where the subjects gave tenth of the produce of the land to their priests and kings. Thus, by faith in God's promise of provision, Jacob vowed to God, that is, the Angel of the Lord, or High Priest of God, tenth of all.

After twenty years of working for Laban, he became exceedingly rich with God's help. Through special breeding of the flocks inspired by God, "...the man (Jacob) increased and became exceedingly rich, and had many sheep and goats, and maidservants, menservants, camels, and donkeys." (Genesis 30:43) At this time the Angel of the Lord appeared again to Jacob and directed him back home:

> I am the God of Bethel, where you anointed the pillar and
> where you vowed a vow to Me. Now arise, get out from
> this land and return to your native land. (Genesis 31:13)

The Angel's reference to the vow in this verse seems to indicate that the vow has not been paid yet. But this is expected, as Jacob promised to pay his vow *after* his safe, peaceful return to his father's house. This would involve God changing his brother's heart.

True to His word, God fulfilled *all* His promises. God made him exceedingly rich and led him safely back home. But strangely, there is no record of him tithing, at least in the Scriptures. Was he being deceptive? Even after a peaceful encounter with Esau (as God changed his heart), when he returned to Bethel, there is no mention of him tithing to God:

> 9 And God [in a distinctly visible manifestation] appeared to Jacob again when he came out of Padan-aram and declared a blessing on him. …
> 11 And God said to him, I am God Almighty. Be fruitful and multiply; a nation and a company of nations shall come from you and kings shall be born of your stock; 12 The land which I gave Abraham and Isaac I will give to you, and to your descendants after you I will give the land. 13 Then God ascended from him in the place where He talked with him. 14 And Jacob set up a pillar (monument) in the place where he talked with [God], a pillar of stone; and he poured a drink offering on it and he poured oil on it. 15 And Jacob called the name of the place where God had talked with him Bethel [house of God]. 16 And they journeyed from Bethel (Gen. 35:14-16a AMP)

He set up a pillar again and called it God's house (as he promised in Genesis 28:22). He poured a drink offering and anointed it with oil, but there is no mention of tithing. Did he pay his tithe later in time? He may have, but we have no record of it in the Bible.

It is worthy of notice that the blessings God reiterates on him and his descendants are completely unconditional – tithe or no tithe. The giving of tenth was Jacob's idea or promise. We conclude that this account describes a one-time vow, whether fulfilled or unfulfilled, and not a practice of tithing as is known today.

Jacob's vow completes all the references to tithing in the Old Testament. Tithing, however, is discussed in the New Testament as well. What does the New Testament teach about tithing?

TITHING: NEW TESTAMENT

New Testament Scriptures on tithing are found in only four places: three verses in the Gospels and one passage in the book of Hebrews. What do they teach? Some teachers hold the argument that the mere mention of tithing in the New Testament is considered proof that tithing applies to us. That reasoning is rather weak, as many other Old Testament concepts are mentioned in the New Testament that do not apply to us today, such as: High Priest, temple (building), the Law, circumcision, Passover, etc. Why is the tithe mentioned? Let's find out.

Matthew 23:23, Luke 11:42, 18:12

> Jesus is speaking:
> Matthew 23:23 Woe to you, scribes and Pharisees, hypocrites! For you pay tithe of mint and anise and cumin, and have neglected the weightier *matters* of the law: justice and mercy and faith. These you ought to have done, without leaving the others undone.
>
> Luke 11:42 But woe to you Pharisees! For you tithe mint and rue and all manner of herbs, and pass by justice and the love of God. These you ought to have done, without leaving the others undone.
>
> Luke 18:11 The Pharisee stood and prayed thus with himself, 'God, I thank You that I am not like other men—extortioners, unjust, adulterers, or even as this tax collector.
>
> Luke 18:12 I fast twice a week; I give tithes of all that I possess.

The Pharisees were the most religious, law-abiding group of Jesus' day. In Matthew 23:23 and Luke 11:42 Jesus has some poignant words to say to them. Luke 18:12 is a self-righteous comment by one of the Pharisees. Clearly, these verses are not instructions on tithing to the

New Testament believer. However, these verses indicate that tithing was very much the practice of the day. Indeed, while Jesus was on earth, the law was in full practice: the temple still stood, and sacrifices were still being made. Zechariah was still fulfilling his high priestly duties, and the Passover was celebrated each year. The Scriptures say that Jesus Himself was born under the Law:

> But when the proper time had fully come, God sent His Son, born of a woman, born subject to [the regulations of] the Law, To purchase the freedom of (to ransom, to redeem, to atone for) those who are subject to the Law, that we might be adopted and have sonship conferred upon us [and be recognized as God's sons]. (Gal. 4:4-5, Amp.)

So, the Law was in place when Jesus began His ministry. Tithing and other practices of the Law continued by Orthodox Jews till the temple was destroyed in 70 A.D. So why was Jesus chastising the Pharisees? Jesus has come to earth with a mission, to both: fulfill and to free us from the Law. I believe that He uses this most religious group to point out man's failure to keep the Law and the need for Him to come and fulfill it. In these verses Jesus brings attention to the fact that serving God involves more than a legalistic and ritualistic observance of the Law. It involves the weightier matters also: of judgment, mercy, faith, and love of God, or in short, a matter of the heart, of which these men were incapable.

He said: "Think not that I am come to destroy the Law, or the prophets: I am not come to destroy, but to fulfill." (Matthew 5:17). He explains:

> Matthew 5:20 For I say unto you, That except your righteousness shall exceed the righteousness of the scribes and Pharisees, ye shall in no case enter into the kingdom of heaven. 5:21 Ye have heard that it was said of them of old time, "Thou shalt not kill; and whosoever shall kill shall be in danger of the judgment:"

47

5:22 But I say unto you, That whosoever is angry with his brother without a cause shall be in danger of the judgment: and whosoever shall say to his brother, "Raca", shall be in danger of the council: but whosoever shall say, "Thou fool", shall be in danger of hell fire....

This is the first of several examples in this passage where Jesus reveals how the outward observance of the Law falls short of God's Law, which Jesus summed up in Luke 10:27: "'You shall love the LORD your God with all your heart, with all your soul, with all your strength, and with all your mind,' and 'your neighbor as yourself.'" Jesus' earthly ministry was to fulfill this law, which was finalized by sacrificially laying down His life for His brethren.

Jesus came to set us free from bondage of sin. He is after our hearts and not ritualistic work. So, tithing by the Pharisees in these verses is no proof that it is mandated for New Testament believers to tithe. On the contrary, the above verses in Galatians show us the "other side of the coin," that Jesus did indeed come to free us from the weight of ritualistic law and to confer sonship upon us through His death and resurrection. Freedom from the Law is the topic of the book of Hebrews in which we find the last passage in the Bible on tithing.

Hebrews 7

The book of Hebrews centers around the exultation of Jesus Christ as: Gods' Holy Son, the perfect, spotless Lamb of God, the new High Priest, and our New Covenant giver. Expressing it in the Apostle Paul's words in his letter to the Corinthians, the book's main theme can be stated as: "Old things have passed away, behold all things have become new" (2 Corinthians 5:17). When Jesus offered Himself as the final, perfect sacrifice for our sins – the only offering acceptable to the Father – a new kind of relationship with God became possible. Instead of observing intricately detailed and numerous ceremonial laws (including tithing) and sacrificing countless animals just to ensure

God's presence, man now is invited into a new, intimate, and eternal relationship with the Godhead. In this relationship man's sins are remembered no more and men and women are affectionately called sons of God.

This new relationship is established under a New Covenant, which assures justification by faith alone in Jesus Christ without any works of the Law or works of our own. The only criterion is that we must believe this incredible exchange – of Jesus receiving the punishment we deserve, while we receive His righteousness – and humbly accept this truth in our hearts. It is a new life for believers today, marked by freedom and forgiveness, with a wonderful result of being able to bear many good fruit through the Holy Spirit Who lives in our hearts.

How would Paul explain to his Jewish readers – the original beneficiaries of the Old Covenant – this change in relationship with God? How could Jesus bring such a change? First, Paul establishes in their understanding that Jesus is the new High Priest and that his High Priestly office is not a continuation of the earthly Levitical priesthood, but of a completely different order. It was bestowed upon Him by God after He defeated death and sin. "For it is attested [by God] of Him, 'You (Christ) are a Priest forever according to the order of Melchizedek.'" (Hebrews 7:17, Amp.) Why was this change in priesthood necessary? The following explains:

> 11 Now if perfection [a perfect fellowship between God and the worshiper] had been attained through the Levitical priesthood (for under it the people were given the Law) what further need was there for another and different kind of priest to arise, one in the manner of Melchizedek, rather than one appointed to the order of Aaron? 12 For when there is a change in the priesthood, there is of necessity a change of the law [concerning the priesthood] as well. 13 For the One of whom these things are said belonged [not to the priestly line of Levi but] to another tribe, from which no one has officiated or served at the altar. 14 For it is

evident that our Lord descended from [the tribe of] Judah, and Moses mentioned nothing about priests in connection with that tribe. 15 And this becomes even more evident if another priest arises in the likeness of Melchizedek, 16 who has become a priest, not on the basis of a physical and legal requirement in the Law [concerning his ancestry as a descendant of Levi], but on the basis of the power of an indestructible and endless life. 17 For it is attested [by God] of Him,

"You (Christ) are a Priest forever According to the order of Melchizedek." (Hebrew 7:11-17, Amp.)

Many mortal, earthly priests, needing forgiveness themselves, got replaced by one, perfect, immortal High Priest Who lives forever. The Old Covenant got replaced with a new one and the High Priest of this New Covenant enables many to come to a saving knowledge of God:

20 And inasmuch as He was not made priest without an oath 21 (for they have become priests without an oath, but He with an oath by Him who said to Him: "The Lord has sworn And will not relent, 'You are a priest forever According to the order of Melchizedek'"), 22 by so much more Jesus has become a surety of a better covenant.
23 Also there were many priests, because they were prevented by death from continuing. 24 But He, because He continues forever, has an unchangeable priesthood. 25 Therefore He is also able to save to the uttermost those who come to God through Him, since He always lives to make intercession for them.

26 For such a High Priest was fitting for us, who is holy, harmless, undefiled, separate from sinners, and has become higher than the heavens; 27 who does not need daily, as those high priests, to offer up sacrifices, first for His own sins and then for the people's, for this He did once for all when He offered up Himself. 28 For the law appoints as high priests men who have weakness, but the word of the oath, which came after the law, appoints the Son who has been perfected forever.

50

To help explain and accept Jesus as the new High Priest by his Jewish readers, Paul uses the tithe. No orthodox Jew, that is a Jew who follows the Law, would recognize a priest outside of the tribe of Levi. But Jesus was from the tribe of Judah, and of a different order from a heavenly perspective. To validate the Scriptures, Paul shows them that Abraham tithed to this High Priest, even before Levi came to existence, whose tribe received tithes from the people:

> Heb. 7:4 Now consider how great this man was, unto whom even the patriarch Abraham gave the tenth of the spoils. 5 And verily they that are of the sons of Levi, who receive the office of the priesthood, have a commandment to take tithes of the people according to the law, that is, of their brethren, though they come out of the loins of Abraham: 6 But he whose descent is not counted from them received tithes of Abraham, and blessed him that had the promises…

> 8 Furthermore, here [in the Levitical priesthood] tithes are received by men who are subject to death; while there [in the case of Melchizedek], they are received by one of whom it is testified that he lives [perpetually]. Amp.

A Jew would associate tithing and priesthood as going hand in hand. Thus, Abraham tithing to Melchizedek is the only proof Paul needs to show that there is another High Priest, not descended from Levi. And, in fact, Levi himself tithed to this man through Abraham: "Even Levi, who receives tithes, paid tithes through Abraham, so to speak, for he was still in the loins of his father when Melchizedek met him." (7:9, 10). As for those who need proof, the Jews, there could be no greater proof of the authenticity of Jesus than Abraham himself tithing to Him. They considered Abraham to be the greatest man, and themselves his descendants.

Upon reading these Scriptures, therefore, it should be clear to the reader that the author of Hebrews has a very specific purpose for mentioning the tithe. It is neither to teach the Gentile believers to tithe nor to encourage the new Jewish converts to continue to tithe. It is to help the Jewish believers understand, through the Abrahamic and Levitical tithes, the change in the priesthood, and consequently in the law.

If the Apostle Paul would have advocated tithing, there would be evidence in the lives of the apostles and disciples tithing. However, there is no such evidence in Scripture, nor of them instructing any of the young churches to tithe. On the contrary, Paul wrote a poignant letter to the Galatians about living by the Law and not by the leading of the Holy Spirit – by grace. He had much to say about imposing the Law on believers in Christ Jesus. He sharply rebuked those Jews who demanded circumcision of all new believers, including Gentiles. He allowed no Law to be imposed whether it be foods to eat or not to eat, observance of Holy Days, etc. Nothing could be added to the grace of Jesus Christ. He didn't even mention the tithe, because in the Jewish mindset it belonged to the Levites, and Jewish leaders did not insist on Gentile Christians tithing (Acts 21:25). He was severely persecuted by his fellow Jews for leading new converts into the freedom of grace, and away from the Law of the letter (See Acts 21:20-21,27ff), though they knew him well as the most religious, zealous, practicing Jew before his conversion.

As a final observation, only Jesus (in the Gospels) and Paul (in Hebrews) mention tithing in the New Testament. Jesus addressed His own people -- the Jews, some of them Pharisees -- according to their own understanding and practices of the Law. The Pharisees Jesus was talking to knew exactly what He meant by tithing – bringing in ten percent of the spices. After His ascension, only the Apostle Paul brought up tithing. He explained to the Jews that tithing, as they knew it, had come to an end, and that they were free from the Law. They were now invited to enter into a New Covenant. With no other mention of the tithe, we find no connection between believers in Christ and tithing, neither in practice nor in instruction.

TITHING: CONCLUSION

All verses in the Bible on the tithe have been discussed and the result is that every mention of the tithe pertains to either the Mosaic tithe, Abraham's tithe, or Jacob's vow. There is no other mention of the tithe in the Bible. What significance did the Mosaic tithe carry?

Tithing was connected to the redemption of man. The tithe represented the need for a mediator – a priesthood -- whose work was indispensable in bringing about forgiveness of sins. In the case of the earthly priesthood, the Levites, regular sacrifices had to be made because the blood of animals could not remove sins. In the case of Jesus, the High Priest, He offered Himself as the sacrificial Lamb, and with that offering He ended the need for further sacrifices. He was the perfect sacrifice acceptable to God.

The tithe signified a necessary separation for God's holy purpose. Thus were the Levites and Christ set apart. Christ was set apart from the foundation of the world for this purpose: to redeem mankind from sin.

As it was a tenth portion that God determined to go to the priesthood, Abraham tithing to the High Priest of his day, possibly the Pre-Incarnate Christ, signified that Jesus is our eternal High Priest. When His task was accomplished, He assumed His role as High Priest forever.

All things in the Old Testament were a shadow of things to come and were pointing to Christ. Jesus put an end to the countless slaughter of animals, the need for an earthly, temporal priesthood, and the associated tithe. The old and temporary passed away. The new has come. Christ is the final fulfillment of all things. Jesus fulfilled the Law. Jesus died and rose again, and we are forever connected to our Heavenly Father through His blood.

With this victorious note the study on tithing has come to an end. Hopefully many questions about tithing have been answered. But surely not all, and important discussions on tithing are yet to follow in the next two sections. The first one is on the principle of tenth.

THE PRINCIPLE OF TENTH

If Christ has redeemed us from our sins and from the Law, then why, we might ask, is tithing taught from the Old Covenant today? The answer in many people's minds, including many respected Bible teachers, is that the Bible holds an important principle: the principle of tenth. From Moses' tithe, Abraham's tithe, and Jacob's vow, it is concluded that tenth of our income belongs to, or should belong to, God.

Naturally, whatever belongs to God we are obliged to pay it. If tenth of what we have, or earn, is God's, then not paying Him is robbing Him, which is a serious offence. Withholding from God ends in negative consequences but paying Him results in blessings. This is basically what is commonly taught from Malachi 3:8-10. Thus, teaching the principle of tenth brings us back to the Law.

To determine whether the principle of tenth applies to us or not, the contexts in which the tenth is applied must be considered. A principle has to be applicable from one context to another. The three examples from which the tenth principle is derived describe no ordinary circumstances. They reflect special provision and special intervention of God. Let us consider each.

In the case of the Israelites, they received instant capital – land, houses, flocks and herd. Basic needs were instantly provided for. The land provided not only initial gain but continuous increase with the recurring harvest. The tenth was easily measurable. It applied in a closed system that began with the Promised Land with defined boundaries. Then it was carefully divided between the tribes and their families. From their apportioned land they returned to God tenth of the harvest and of the increase of the animals. The picture describes a system where tithing was equally applicable and equally manageable to all. The tithe, the land, the nation and all things pertaining to these, such as the priesthood, were holy – sacred – set apart for the Lord. God's manifest presence was with the Israelites as He dwelt among them.

In the case of Abraham, he found himself going to war against four kings and their armies with only 318 of his trained men. These four kings and their armies were so powerful that even five kings and their armies could not defeat them. Yet, Abraham defeated them with his 318 men, and recovered all the belongings of two towns (Sodom and Gomorrah). Keeping the spoil for himself would have constituted a major wealth transfer for him. This supernatural increase came by the hand of God. God showed up in the battle and in the person of the High Priest, Melchizedek, to whom Abraham gave tenth of all the spoil, and the rest he returned to the kings.

Jacob encountered God in many unique ways. As pertaining to the offering of tenth to God, he gained vast amount of wealth by God's supernatural intervention. God caused Jacob's flock and herd to multiply supernaturally, and thereby transfer of wealth from Laban to Jacob. The Bible says that Jacob became very wealthy. Of this, Jacob offered tenth to the Lord. God's manifest presence was with Jacob and enabled him to thrive according to God's predetermined plan.

We could hardly call these three cases ordinary. They tithed from increase that came by God's special intervention and provision. They did not tithe from earned income they worked for to make a living or attain possessions. They simply returned tenth of what God Himself attained for them.

If we think of the Israelites, they surely had income apart from the farm – life required more than growing food, such as practicing trades. In fact, their income most likely would not have come from the farm, as all had lands from which they were required to tithe and feed their households. So, there would have been no one to sell their harvest to.

Whatever money they made on the side, God did not require them to tithe on it, but on tenth of what God gave them: the land. *This tithe* was holy unto the Lord.

Obviously, tithing on the land they acquired does not compare with tithing on income today. One is tithing on increase, and the other on income, which are not the same, as will be explained in detail later. If the Mosaic tithe does not fit the context today, Abraham's tithe does even less. From the biblical account, he tithed only once when the High Priest showed up. How can we surmise regular giving of earned income from this one account?

Jacob's tenth has even less "leg to stand on." We don't even know if he ever fulfilled his promise, and if so, we don't know how. Who did he give his tithe to? We do not know anything about the events surrounding his promised tithe. All we know is that he promised God to give Him tenth of what He gained for him *after* he returned to his father's house. That means he did not tithe for at least 20 years. How can we draw a principle of tithing tenth of income from this account? Are we not presumptuous in building a doctrine on just a portion?

It is Abraham's tithe that takes the argument for tithing today, since the Mosaic Law has passed away. That argument is very weak as stated above. But the principle of tenth is still connected to the word "tithe," which takes us back to the Mosaic Law. Let us see how this path leads us down the wrong road.

An interesting observation was made earlier in this book. It was that there are several Hebrew words that mean "tenth," and all are translated as "tenth," except two: *"mahasar"* and *"asar,"* which are translated as "tithe." Curiosity was raised as to why this was so. A clue is gained when we realize that these Hebrew words were used exclusively with Moses's tithe, Abraham's tithe, and Jacob's vow. These instances refer to God's special selection of people and nation. They were part of God's holy plan. The tithe was not just tenth of anything.

56

We gather from the Word that *"mahasar"* is "holy" – set apart for God. Leviticus 27:30, 32 states: "...all the *tithe* (*mahasar*) of the land, whether of the seed of the land or of the fruit of the tree, *is the Lord's. It is holy to the Lord...*" As we read this, we observe that it does not say that "tenth" is holy, but that the "tithe" is holy. The tithe includes in its meaning "tenth," but it is more than just "tenth." The "tithe of the land" was not equivalent to "tenth of the land" – which would imply tenth of the physical land – but tenth of what the land produced, or "increase of the land." *This* tenth is what God called as *holy* to Himself. The distinction between "tenth" and "tithe" is clearly seen here.

Tenth, as the portion, must be measurable. Before a portion can be determined, the "whole" must be clearly known. With the Israelites, the "whole" represented the Promised Land – a specific area of land with defined boundaries. It was a free gift and free capital to be divided among the tribes. The tribes and families were equally blessed. After the land was divided, the apportioned land became the "whole" from which the families returned to God tenth of the harvest and of the increase of the animals. The tithe was easily measurable. The picture describes a closed system where tithing was equally applicable and equally manageable to all.

Being holy, *"mahasar"* required further specification: who it was for, who was to pay it, when, how, how often and where. When a Jew heard the word "tithe" he had to know all these details. The word was "loaded" as we would say today. Everything to know about the holy tithe was in the name.

Holiness characterized Abraham's tithe (*mahasar*) as well. Only after the High Priest Melchizedek showed up with bread and wine and blessed Abraham, did Abraham tithe to him. Like the Law required later, he tithed on increase that came by a supernatural intervention of God and he tithed to the High Priest.

Tenth is just a simple portion. Could a portion "tenth," without any context, be a principle? Can it be designated as "holy," and does the Bible do so? The answers are, "No!" I believe that the foundational problem with the principle of tenth, and the source of confusion over tithing today, is the assumption, or a mistaken understanding, that tithe means simply tenth. "Tithe" and "tenth" are two different terms both in Hebrew and in English. The tithe is tithe and tenth is tenth. To reduce the "tithe" to just "tenth" is to strip it of its context – the very context that makes it holy.

Once "tenth" becomes "holy," whatever we attach to it becomes "holy." Recognizing that the Mosaic tithe does not apply to us today, we "re-dress" the "tenth" with "income" and conclude that "tenth of income" is "holy." Yes, it is so preached by some today: tenth of our income – money – is "holy to the Lord." Following the blueprint of Malachi 3:8-10, this "holy tithe" is labeled as belonging to God, belonging to the local church (the storehouse). Paying or not paying it invites blessings or curses into our lives.

Should the Bible even just imply the principle of tenth, and the corresponding "tenth of income" as "holy," there should be at least some mention of it somewhere in the Bible. Yet, in searching the Word for "income," we find no result anywhere in the Bible. The biblical term and concept associated with the biblical tithe is not "income" but "increase." These two terms are not the same and are not interchangeable. A discussion on how they are different will follow in the next chapter.

If "income" is not found in the Bible, certainly "tenth" or "ten percent" would be mentioned some way in the New Testament, since the key word in the principle of tenth is "tenth." Particularly important would be to find these words in books written to Gentile Christians, since Gentiles were not familiar with biblical tithing. (The word "tithe" was already examined and was determined that it appeared with reference to the Mosaic and Abrahamic tithes.) Searching for "ten" and "tenth" in the New Testament brings up no result pertaining to giving. The principle of tenth does not appear in the New Testament. If we struggle with this thought, let us ask a probing question.

If the tenth of all our income belongs to God, would it not have been negligent of the disciples not to teach their new converts to regularly give these to God? The consequences of resulting curses for robbing God, as some teach, would have fallen on the disciples' heads. Also, if tithing was critical to incur God's many blessings (particularly financial prosperity) as is taught today, would it not have been inconsiderate, not to mention negligent, of the apostles to not tell their followers about it?

It would have been particularly important to teach the Gentile believers to tithe – or give a tenth of their income – who would not have been familiar with biblical tithing. Surely, we would find at least one sermon in the New Testament about giving of tenth. Yet we find no evidence of any of the apostles, disciples, or followers of Christ tithing or giving tenth, or teaching the new converts to do the same. This explains why tithing and the principle of tenth is taught – and can only be taught – from the Old Testament.

The pursuit of "tenth" causes a subtle but profound change in focus on giving. Instead of a principle of giving or sharing, or giving to God, the portion "tenth" gets elevated. In pursuit of tenth, teaching this principle has led us back to the Law, or at least a doctrine of requirement, which is in effect a law.

What happens when we strip away the context and reduce the meaning of the tithe to just the portion tenth? Once the principle of tenth is embraced, it opens the door to re-interpret Scripture. Thus, the Mosaic tithe in Malachi 3:8-10 is completely redefined and the whole passage re-interpreted. The intention by the preacher is to teach people the benefit of giving and to urge them to give, but the teaching is laden with man-made assumptions. The tithe (*mahasar*) becomes money earned,

59

designated as "holy," to be paid to the church – an institution that needs the money for more things than just *feeding people* (the true tithe) – and blessings and curses follow tithers/non-tithers.

Unquestionably, Malachi 3:8-10 is misrepresented and taught out of context today. This "new" doctrine on tithing may be the only doctrine Christians are familiar with, yet it is nowhere found in the Bible. This understanding is so imbedded in the body of Christ, that one may find hard to believe the true nature of the biblical tithe.

Does the Bible allow for such liberty? Probably the most serious aspect of this teaching, and I believe the main source of confusion over tithing today, is that the term "tithe" has not been changed. That is, the holy tithe of Malachi 3:8-10 has been completely redefined yet continues to be called "tithe." This can be deceiving. The believers today only hear that the tithe in this passage is tenth of income and that it belongs to God. Do we have jurisdiction to change the holy tithe – which *God* called holy – to something else? To state that anything belongs to God, and that it is holy, when God did not say so, is misrepresenting His Word, to say the least. Have those of us who teach this doctrine been unintentionally caught up in hidden deception through misrepresenting the Word? For this will God hold them accountable?

From a practical perspective, let us ponder the following thoughts. Can tenth of income in an open system, like the world at large, replace the biblical tithe? Could we say we all have inherited equal assets and that we all have equal paying jobs to make tithing fair? Of course not, and there are plenty of poor in our world today. How are the poor protected? The principle of tenth requires everyone to give ten percent of their income to God. Does that compare to the Mosaic tithe where the landowner paid his tithe for his household, but not each member of the household paid it? Further, of those who had no land, not only did they not pay any tithes, but they themselves were the recipients of a tithe. Comparisons come short in every aspect, which are many, and it is safe to conclude that a simple principle of tenth cannot be deducted from the Mosaic tithe, not to mention, from Abraham's tithe and Jacob's vow.

What if the key principle derived from the tithe is not the portion "tenth" but the principle of giving to God? We are a new creation in Christ, filled with His Spirit, His love and His heart. He leads and guides us, and we must trust His guidance in giving. We might consider the tenth as a symbol for giving to God, but which can be any amount He Himself directs and guides us to give. Giving from the heart of God and from one's own heart is what pleases Him.

Teaching the Holy and Supreme Word of God is a formidable task. None of us, who love God with our whole hearts, want to misrepresent it. On the contrary, we want to bring everything out of it so we can live by and tell others about it. The Bible is not an easy book to understand, and requires the Holy Spirit, the Author, to reveal it to us. After much study, I perceive that teaching tithing from Malachi creates a number of problems with reference to misrepresenting Scripture. The following chapter expounds on this.

CHALLENGES WITH TEACHING TITHING FROM MALACHI 3:8-10

> Malachi 3:8-10: "Will a man rob God? Yet you have robbed Me! But you say, 'In what way have we robbed You?' In tithes and offerings. 9 You are cursed with a curse, For you have robbed Me, Even this whole nation. 10 Bring all the tithes into the storehouse, That there may be food in My house, And try Me now in this," Says the Lord of hosts, "If I will not open for you the windows of heaven And pour out for you such blessing That there will not be room enough to receive it. (NKJV)

This passage is widely preached by many Christian ministries. The promise of great blessings is their key message for faithfully paying tenth of one's income to God, with a warning of consequences if one does not pay the tithe, which would be curses over one's life. What challenges do preachers face when they teach tithing from this passage?

Teaching the Passage out of Context

It's been stated and cannot be overemphasized how important context is. Let us ask these questions as we read this passage: Who are these highly emotional and intense words directed to? "You" is a very personal address. Who is God speaking to? Is He speaking to all of humanity? Is this charge universal? The previous two verses tell clearly:

> 6 For I am the Lord, I do not change; Therefore you are not consumed, O sons of Jacob. 7 Yet from the days of your fathers You have gone away from My ordinances And have not kept them. Return to Me, and I will return to you," Says the Lord of hosts. "But you said, 'In what way shall we return?' (Malachi 3:6-7)

The people God was addressing were the sons of Jacob. The message was highly specific and personal. They knew and understood exactly what God required of them and how they had failed Him. To us today, frankly, verses 8-10 make no sense at all. Yet, without explaining the context, the passage is usually read in such a way as to make it personal to us. Thus comes the charge of God from the pulpit against those who may not be tithing ten percent of their income: "you have robbed Me!" "You are cursed with a curse." Conversely, to those who have been tithing, God's promises are boldly proclaimed: "I will ... open for you the windows of heaven and pour out for you such blessing that there will not be room enough to receive it."

In this passage everything hinges on God's specific instructions, which include the specifics pertaining to the tithe. To preach the same content to anyone else is taking the passage out of context. The results can be false charges and accusations:

"You have robbed Me!"

To rob is to take away, sometimes forcefully, something from someone that clearly belongs to them. Using such a strong word not only expresses the way God feels about it but implies that the "act" was done intentionally – with full understanding that they were taking away from God what rightfully belonged to Him.

What did *we* rob God of? Does the New Testament teach that ten percent of our income belongs to God? The answer was given in the previous chapter – no. Tenth of income is not even mentioned in the New Testament. As Malachi 3:8-10 is taken out of context, this false charge against believers in Christ naturally follows.

"You are cursed with a curse":

Being charged with robbing God is bad enough but pronouncing a curse on God's children is clearly unbiblical. Christ's blood acquits us: "Christ has redeemed us from the curse of the law." (Galatians 3:13).

Besides the clear Word on this subject – that Christ removed the curse from us – let us also look deeper into Malachi 3:8-10. God told His people "You are cursed with a curse," but then He also told them what to do to undo the curse: "bring all the tithes into the storehouse...." How did bringing their tithes change the course of being under a curse? This reminder puts it into perspective:

The tithes related to man's relationship with God. When Jesus hung on the cross and became a curse for us, thereby restoring man's relationship with God apart from the works of the law, relationship was forever established for a child of God. Failure to do everything right does not cut us off from God and put us back under a curse. The curse entails everything that happens when God is not there. As an earthly father does not leave or disown his child when he or she does wrong, even if they willfully disobey, likewise, our Heavenly Father will not leave or disown us. Rather, Jesus declared: "I will never leave you nor forsake you." (Hebrews 13:5) However, discipline does follow undesirable behavior to a legitimate child, as we read in Hebrews chapter 12:3-11. To even use the word or concept of "curse" for a child of God is seriously undermining not only the Word of God, but the finished, sacrificial work of Christ on the cross. It also reveals a profound lack of understanding of the grace of God. In Christ we are gloriously blessed (Ephesians 1:3)! Unless a child of God deliberately turns his back on the Father and chooses to sever that relationship, he is not under a curse anymore.

Under the Law they had to keep tithing and sacrificing to ensure God's presence and protection from all curses. This concept has crept into many sermons today when we hear that, literally, all blessings in life originate from paying one's tithes, and misfortunes (curses) follow those who do not tithe. This is the result of preaching from the Law. As long as we preach *from* the Law, we preach law.

Misusing the Term Tithe

The central message of *God's heart for Giving* pertains to this: the misuse of the term tithe. What we call tithing today and what the Bible calls tithing are two different things. How did we arrive at what is taught today? The root of the discrepancy is found in the meaning of the "tithe." The Hebrew word translated as "tithe" basically means tenth. This is what is known by all. But tenth is just a portion and is meaningless by itself. Tenth can be of anything, so it must be defined what it is tenth of. The Bible quite specifically defines what it is. Whenever the word "tithe" appears in the Bible, it will be related to either Abraham's tithe or the tithe instituted under the Law of Moses. In addition, "tenth" appears in connection with Jacob' vow. In all these Scriptures the tithe has a meaning. Ultimately, the meaning is: *tenth of increase*. In Abraham's case, it was tenth of spoil. In the nation Israel's case, it was tenth of increase of land and of herd or flock. In Jacob's case, it was vowed to be tenth of all he received from God after a certain period of time when many conditions were met.

64

Not fully realizing the significance of the word "increase," or not understanding its meaning, the tithe is automatically understood as, and is taught to mean, "ten percent of income" today. Is ten percent of income the same as tenth of increase? Increase and income may sound the same, and at first may imply the same, but they are very different, particularly when applied in different contexts. Let us take a closer look at each.

Increase vs Income

Before tithing could and did begin, the tribes acquired great possessions of land, animals, houses, and all things necessary. Whether Abraham, Jacob, or the tribes of Israel, they all boasted of *ownership* of great possessions before tithing took place. Of the tribes it is written:

> 10 So it shall be, when the Lord your God brings you into the land of which He swore to your fathers, to Abraham, Isaac, and Jacob, to give you large and beautiful cities which you did not build, 11 houses full of all good things, which you did not fill, hewn-out wells which you did not dig, vineyards and olive trees which you did not plant ... (Deuteronomy 6:10-11, NKJV)

Thus, when the tribes entered the Promised Land, they began life with possession of basic assets: land, livestock, houses, and goods. Tithing began as the land produced its yield and as the flock and herd multiplied. The tithes were to be brought into the storehouse once a year, and the increase of animals three times a year. Tithing was on increase only. For example, Leviticus 27:32 reads: "And concerning the tithe of the herd or the flock, of whatever passes under the rod, the tenth one shall be holy to the Lord." Thus, when the flock owner counted the animals of the increase in the flock, if there were nine or fewer in increase, there was nothing to tithe. If his increase was 29 animals, he was obligated to tithe two animals. What if the increase was only one animal? No tithe was required. Until an increase of ten animals, no tithe was required.

65

Were the tribes required to tithe on income from other labor? This question was answered with a resounding "No!" earlier in the book. But going along with the concept of "income," the following discussion shows how it could not have logistically worked. The dictionary definition of income is: "the monetary payment received for goods or services, or from other sources, as rents or investments." The key words are *"monetary payment."* Money serves as a medium of exchange. Tithing *on income* would mean tithing *on money* received for goods or services or labor.

Tithing on income becomes problematic when money is not used as a medium of exchange. For example, trading and bartering were common in early Israel's history as a way to meet basic needs. A fabric maker might swap his fabric with a tailor who sewed his clothes, for example. Goods and services provided basic needs for self and others. How would they tithe on such an exchange? No tithing could be done. Basic needs were to be met, and God did not ask them to tithe on basic needs and necessities. For example, He did not say to them: "I want you to stop bartering and sell what you make for money, and charge money for all your services. Add up what you make every month, and ten percent of that set aside for the Levites. I am giving this money to them as their inheritance for the service they do for you in the Tabernacle." Of course, God did not say that, and this thinking is not reflective neither of the tithe He instituted nor of His heart. This scenario depicts more a God who takes away from His people the product of their labor, than a God Who gives. God did not take ownership of what man labored for. He did not require ten percent of their "income." God did ask for free-will offerings, but these were not to be confused with the tithe.

In today's society, money is almost exclusively used as a medium of exchange for goods and services. This money represents all sorts of basic needs a person buys with it. Unlike the Israeli tribes who instantly inherited land and all other property, most people today do not own

66

land, a home, their car(s), and possibly other things they use. Much income is spent on just paying off loans on things they should own. In addition, many of our regular financial obligations are not "own-able," such as: taxes (on income, house, car), insurances (on car, home, health), gas for car, utilities, phone services, internet, etc. What is left may barely cover food and other necessary items for some families, especially for larger families or individuals with lesser income. *Income* today is not equivalent to *increase* in Israel's economic system.

What might tithing on the increase look like in a modern-day example? The following illustration helps explain. Suppose a father gives his son his inheritance when he becomes of age: a nice house with all its furnishings on ten acres of land, a car, and a well-established, successful business. All employees are fully in place in the business and all he has to do is to run it. The only thing the father withholds from the son is ten percent of the business' net income. From it he wants a particular Christian ministry to be funded. The business is in the son's possession, yet he cannot spend ten percent of the increase in any way he wants to but must follow his father's direction. Should the business not bring in a net income, the son does not tithe. When it does, the father wants ten percent to be donated to his select Christian ministry. Should the son start another business, what he does with the increase is totally up to him. The father has no say in it. He may ask his father for advice, but all is up to him.

Therefore, when God charged the sons of Jacob with robbing Him of the tithe in Malachi 3:8, He did not pronounce them cursed for robbing Him of tenth of their income, but for robbing Him of the tithe He instituted. These two "tithes" are not the same. To assume anything else for the tithe than what was instituted, and preach the consequences attributed to the biblical tithe is seriously misrepresenting God's Word. Mixing and matching biblical terms and concepts with our ideas does not only result in mishandling God's Word but in causing confusion and fear.

The question to ponder is, should we even use the term "tithe" today? If the apostles, disciples, and writers of the New Testament did not use this term for giving, should we? All of them, being Jews, knew very well what the tithe stood for. So, they expressed giving in terms of "giving alms," "sowing," "giving charity," or just "giving." Should we not follow suit? Another familiar term we can use today is "offerings." Interestingly, the Jews do not use the term "tithing" in their synagogues today either. They use the term "dues."

When we regularly use the term "tithing" for giving, we inevitably preach ten percent, and in most peoples' minds it conjures up obligatory giving, and with it fear, guilt and condemnation should they not be able to pay it. There is nothing wrong with giving ten percent on a regular basis. In fact, it is a wonderful goal. But so are 11 percent, 9 percent, 20 percent and 5 percent and any other percent a person is able and willing to pay; they are all wonderful goals. To choose not to use the term "tithe," one does not say to stop giving. The goal is for everyone to understand that God lays no obligation of any certain amount, and His only requirement is that we give cheerfully, liberally, and not grudgingly. Much more discussion on how to give, how much, when, etc., follows in Parts II and III of this book.

This thesis so far should have brought a clear understanding of the dilemma we face: the tithe of the Bible and what we call tithing today are two different things. We have exchanged the meaning of the biblical tithe with another meaning. This "simple," unpretentious move has bigger implications than we may realize, as has been partially shown and continues to be explored.

Misrepresenting the Purpose of the Tithe

If we were asked to explain or define the purpose of tithing today, what would we say? Some would say that it is the key to financial prosperity. Others feel that the tithe is holy and belongs to God. What does "belongs to God" mean? How does it belong to Him? What does He do with it? What is the tithe's ultimate purpose? The most common answer one hears today is that the tithe belongs to the local church from where the kingdom of God is advanced. How is the tithe money used in the church? Though church budgets vary, tithes typically cover building and operational expenses, salaries, church ministries, missions, other ministries, helping the needy, etc. While these expenditures are necessary for the church to survive and to thrive, they should not be confused with the biblical tithe.

What was the purpose of the biblical tithe when it was instituted? The answer is very simple – to feed the Levites, the owner's family, and the poor. The tithe also was the Levites' inheritance, as we know. This is important to state each time, so we don't confuse the tithe with general giving today, which is optional. To stay true to the Malachi passage, from where tithing is taught, the purpose of the tithe should be rightly represented. The tithe in the Bible was food, and building expenses were covered from other offerings. When the Tabernacle was built, for example, special free-will offerings were taken up:

> 25:1 And the LORD spake unto Moses, saying, 25:2 Speak unto the children of Israel, that they bring me an offering: of every man that giveth it willingly with his heart ye shall take my offering. 25:3 And this is the offering which ye shall take of them; gold, and silver, and brass.

Building the Tabernacle did not come from tithe "money." Buying or renting a building and running an organization today is not the problem, but the designation of the funds is. When the tithe is presented as "holy," "belonging to God," etc., and then is spent to cover building and operational expenses, these – building and operational expenses – in essence, are sanctioned as "holy," and their funding as worthy of incurring blessings, or curses if one does not tithe.

So, let us take the example of a single mother with children, or a family man with many dependents. Most people do not have a six-digit income. Thus, a family, who is struggling to keep food on the table, when required to tithe, might literally be exchanging the children's food and necessities for a building program or for utilities at the church. A biblical way to view this scenario is that since the tithe was food, the parents are "paying their tithes" to God by feeding their children.

Failure to understand what the tithe was (which was of increase), and why it was instituted (to feed the Levites, one's family, and the poor), can bring about gross misrepresentation of not only God's Holy Word, but of God's character. As is taught according to the prosperity gospel, if a father with a large family does not pay his tithe, he misses out on God's many promised blessings, at best, or, at worst, will incur curses upon himself and on his family for robbing God. Contrasting this to people who can easily pay their tithes (whether they have no dependents or have much greater income), they would enjoy not only the promised blessings for tithing, but an additional 30-60-100-fold return on any additional offering beyond the tithe (as preached from Mark 4)! This scenario is neither representative of the biblical tithe nor of the heart of God.

The "ten-percent-for-all" principle or rule can actually cause much fear and tremendous pressure and burden on those people who are struggling to feed and clothe their families. On the other hand, it can create false confidence and pride in those who have a lot of money and who feel like they have fulfilled their obligation to God with an amount they may not even notice as being gone. This perspective can create a very unhealthy view of God – that He is uncaring and only wants our money. What other way is the tithe misrepresented today?

Missing the True Meaning of Holiness

The Bible says that the tithe was holy (Leviticus 27:30). From this verse is taught today that tenth of income is holy and belongs to God. Without carefully considering what it was tenth of, the portion tenth gets to be sanctified. The biblical tithe (according to its full definition) was declared holy, not because it was tenth, but because it was set apart by God for His purpose.

When we single out a portion of something, such as tenth, as holy (set apart), a natural tendency is to think that ninety percent is not holy. The biblical tithe does not refer to partial consecration, but to a distribution of inheritances. The *whole* land was holy to the Lord. The *whole* nation of Israel was set apart from the rest of the nations and was declared holy to the Lord. The tenth only referred to the way the harvest was divided among all the people of the land – twelve tribes, plus the Levites - one tenth of the produce of the total harvest God determined to be the Levites' fair share. Due to the Levites' consecration to temple service, an ordinance had to be made to define their portion and to ensure they received it. The tribe of Levi, the priesthood, and the many other things set apart as holy, were completely, 100 percent, set apart for God. We read about no partial consecration of anything.

So, when we consider the phrase "the tithe was holy" we should focus more on the "holy" part, and ask: "Why was the tithe holy? The Scripture says that it was set apart for the Levites. Why was there need for the Levites? They were God's instruments as mediators between Himself and the people. Once we understand that when Jesus became our Perfect Mediator and new High Priest, the Levites, the tithe, and the offerings lost their purposes. And the concept of tenth derived from the law, passed with the law.

While the portion "tenth" has, therefore, lost its relevance, the concept of holiness is very relevant to the believer in Christ. The Greek word translated "holy" and "saint" is "*hagios*" (*Strong's*, #40) and it means: "*sacred* (pure, blameless, consecrated): - (most) *holy, saint,*" and it occurs 337 times in the King James version of the New Testament! In the Old Testament, references to holy things add up to about 441! Considering that the content of the New Testament is less than one third of the Old, "holy" occurs about three times more frequently in the New than in the Old Testament! How is that for significance?!

71

What is considered holy under the New Covenant? In the Old Testament, besides the nation and priesthood, holy (set apart) things pertained to *things* like the temple and all its furnishings, the altar, sacrifice, ointment, convocation, habitation, Sabbath, place, garment, atonement, animals, the tithe, etc. What holy *things* do we find in the New Testament? None.

Out of the 337 references to holy or holiness, about two thirds (over 200) refer to the *believers*, who are called "saints" (62 times) and are challenged to holy living (over 140 times). Beyond these, 93 times the word refers to the Holy Spirit and the rest of the times to Jesus being holy. If we consider that all things pertaining to the Old Testament Law were a shadow of things to come and pointing to Jesus, *we*, *who are in Jesus*, have become with Him **all** that is **holy**. Thus, **we are** His *holy temple* (1 Corinthians 3:16-17, 6:19-20, Ephesians 2:21), His *holy nation* (1 Peter2:9) and His *holy priesthood* (1 Peter 2:5); *consecrated for pure and holy living* (1 Thessalonians 4:3, 5:23) and challenged to become *holy sacrifices* (Romans 12:1). We are literally His Holy Temple in which He lives.

This subject of holiness brings to light the magnificent changes from the Old to the New Covenant. In the Old Testament, many *things* were holy, while in the New Testament we only read about *people* and God being holy. With this discovery, one wonders why we do not hear more sermons on believers being holy. Thankfully, our righteousness in Christ is gaining more prevalence in sermons with a greater appreciation for and understanding of it. But when it comes to holiness, based on the sermons I was exposed to during the last two or three decades, if I heard the term "holy" it was mostly limited to the "holy tithe."

Such teaching that emphasizes the tithe being holy, but excludes the believer being holy, gives the impression that: (1) the only holy thing in our lives is money, (2) that holiness can be reduced to one tenth – one tenth of our income, and (3) that only part of us is, or required to be, dedicated to the Lord, and not our whole being. In the New Testament, however, there is no such concept that only ten percent, or half, or any portion of us, or what we have, is holy.

As Christ has purchased us with His blood, we are His – not just a portion of our income. Our whole lives are His possession. **We are** set apart for Him. We are holy and must present all we are and all we have to Him as His and holy. "Now may the God of peace Himself sanctify you *completely*; and may your *whole* spirit, soul, and body be preserved blameless at the coming of our Lord Jesus Christ" (1 Thessalonians 5:23, NKJV).

As the Israelites were set apart among all the nations, and the Levites among the tribes, the believers in Christ are also set apart (holy) ones among the nations, representing first fruits: "And it was of His own [free] will that He gave us birth [as sons] by [His] Word of Truth, so that we should be a kind of firstfruits of His creatures [a sample of what He created to be consecrated to Himself]." (James 1:18, AMP). We are the Levites today, so to speak, among the nations. We are His holy priesthood. While we are a portion of nations, our calling to holiness is 100 percent – not ten percent. To say that ten percent of our income is holy (set apart) has no biblical support.

God is looking for total surrender and a totally consecrated life. Focusing on money pertaining to holiness can be very deceiving. Today, incredible promises and emphases have been connected to paying one's tithes. Just about every area of life, including receiving one's healing, or relatives being saved, and other blessings in life have been associated with paying one's tithes. But let us, as an example, consider consecration expressed by families who choose to have many children. Raising many children is one of the most consecrated and self-sacrificing things a person can do. If holiness is determined by paying one's tithes, these families may fare the worst, as they may have the least money to give.

If we focus on the tenth of income, we miss the true meaning of holiness. First, we sanctify money, then the portion, then the act of giving of money. According to the teaching this book is addressing, as long as one gives, regardless of how the money is used, blessings are promised to flow. But failure to give dries up the blessings and curses follow.

Now, giving *can be* a sign of one's consecration to God. A totally surrendered and consecrated life will be evident by one's generous giving. Giving is at the core of God's essence and it will characterize every true believer. But giving can take on many forms. God gave His Son. Parents give to their children a home, food, clothing, and protection. Some people care for the disabled or the elderly. Others give a listening ear, compassion, mercy, and their time. What we give, and to whom, are all part of giving.

Now, admittedly, it is good to "hang onto" some principle on giving. Perhaps the principle drawn from the tithe could be a commitment to give to God a certain portion that a person feels comfortable with after consulting the Lord in prayer. This would be a workable principle that would not contradict the Word of God.

The essence and purpose for tithing was not about the amount tenth, but on the recipients. The tithe was instituted with the recipients in mind. How can we draw a principle from this truth? Who should be the recipients of our committed portion to God? There is no more Levitical priesthood. All believers have become the royal priesthood of God. We still have the poor – the orphans, widows and "strangers" (others in need) in the land. The best sources to find the answers are Jesus' and the Apostles' teachings in the New Testament.

The next section, Part II, turns to New Testament Scriptures on giving. The passages chosen are the ones most frequent found in prosperity sermons. It so happens that these very Scriptures hold the key to giving. What does God teach about giving? Who should give, to whom, what, when, how much, how often, and why?

PART II: GIVING IN THE NEW TESTAMENT

THE SHIFT IN THE COVENANTS

The New Testament introduces the New Covenant God made with man through the shed blood of Jesus, God's Son. The changes from the Old Covenant to the New are drastic. All perspectives change.

The New Testament describes the advent of Christ, namely, God coming to earth to live among men again. Unlike in the Old Testament where God showed Himself as a King, Ruler, Sovereign, Warrior, Provider, and Protector of the Nation, in the New Testament God shows up as a Suffering Servant. He comes to set up His Kingdom in people's hearts. His kingdom will eventually be on the earth, but presently it is in peoples' hearts who believe in Him as their Saviour and thereby become God's children. His mandates to His children today are very different from that of the Israelites'. They are not about building a nation but building a kingdom. They are not to hold one nation together and in the presence of God by numerous sacrifices and ordinances, but to bring all nations into the kingdom of Christ. They are not to collect wealth, but to bless others. They are not just to feed the poor of their own land, but of other nations, and clothe the naked, heal the sick, preach the gospel, heal the brokenhearted, preach deliverance to the captives, recover sight to the blind, and set at liberty them that are bruised.

If the Israeli nation offered tithes and offerings back to God, what do the disciples of Christ have to offer back to God? Jesus gave it all. He is calling His followers to do the same. Jesus represents God's heart. He *is* God's heart. If we are born again, we have His heart. This means we do not follow formalities and rituals of a law, but His heart.

The New Testament tells us that Jesus has fulfilled the requirements of the Law. Christ brought a new system of living – by grace, through

faith, and in the power of the Holy Spirit. Fulfilling the law of Christ –
of loving the Lord our God with all our hearts, minds, and souls, and of
loving our neighbor as ourselves – is not to be fulfilled under the
confinements of any law, or under compulsion, but in the power of His
Holy Spirit Who lives in us and guides us. Tithing has been replaced
with Spirit-led giving under grace. Giving has **not** come to an end.

PASSAGES ON GIVING

The ultimate goal of this study in the New Testament is to find God's
heart about giving. What does *He* want us to know about why give, to
whom, what, how much, when, in what manner, how often, and so on?
Like looking for treasure, we want Him to reveal to us through the Holy
Spirit what He wants us to know, not what we think or makes sense to
us or want to believe.

Prosperity teaching brings attention to some key passages on giving but
presents them in the spirit of the message: the prosperity of the believer.
Thus, the purpose for giving, as for the purpose for tithing, is to gain
God's favor so that He can shower us with financial blessings. Not
surprisingly, the selected passages all have to do with sowing, reaping
and prosperity. They are Luke 6:38, 2 Corinthians 8:9, 9:6-7, Galatians
6:7, Philippians 4:19, Mark 4:1-20 and 3 John 2.

Before any of these passages were written, John the Baptist preached a
sermon on giving. This is not a sermon often heard, but I believe it
beautifully sets the stage on giving in the rest of the New Testament.

John the Baptist

Before Jesus came to earth, bringing the kingdom of heaven with Him,
much preparation was required, particularly in man's heart. John the
Baptist was chosen by God to prepare the way for Jesus and His new
heavenly kingdom on earth. So, John was sent out by God to preach

repentance and to baptize people into repentance. One day, some Pharisees and Sadducees came to be baptized by him. Questioning their hearts, he proposed a challenge to them:

> 8 Therefore bear fruits worthy of repentance, and do not begin to say to yourselves, 'We have Abraham as our father.' For I say to you that God is able to raise up children to Abraham from these stones. 9 And even now the ax is laid to the root of the trees. Therefore, every tree which does not bear good fruit is cut down and thrown into the fire." 10 So the people asked him, saying, "What shall we do then?" 11 He answered and said to them, *"He who has two tunics, let him give to him who has none; and he who has food, let him do likewise."* (Luke 3:8-11, italics added)

Verse 3:11, the one in italics, happens to be the first recorded instruction, the first advice, and the first sermon, so to speak, in the New Testament. It also happens to contain a key revelation to the first step necessary to prepare one's heart for the kingdom Jesus came to establish in people's hearts on earth. What was this first of all instructions? What was this first step in preparation for the kingdom, and a fruit worthy of repentance? It was to *share* one's goods with the poor; to give to the needy; and because even two items were to be shared, it was to bring general equality (2 Corinthians 8:12-15). Will this be the theme of the rest of the New Testament?

Sermon on the Mount
Luke 6:20-38

> Give, and it will be given to you: good measure, pressed down, shaken together, and running over will be put into your bosom. For with the same measure that you use, it will be measured back to you. (Luke 6:38)

This verse may win the medal for being the most frequently quoted verse on giving. Who is to give? To whom? What? When? How? How much? How often? Why? None of these questions can be answered from this verse alone so we must turn to the larger context. The context happens to be the Sermon on the Mount. Preached by Jesus Himself, this sermon reveals much about kingdom living and the heart of God.

After spending all night in prayer on the mountain, Jesus called His disciples and appointed twelve of them to be apostles. Their descent from the mountain was met by a huge crowd who came from all Judea, Jerusalem and the seacoast of Tyre and Sidon, to hear Him and to be cured of their diseases (Luke 6:12-19). Then, we read:

> 20 He lifted up His eyes toward His disciples, and said: "Blessed are you poor, For yours is the kingdom of God. 21 Blessed are you who hunger now, For you shall be filled. Blessed are you who weep now, For you shall laugh. 22 Blessed are you when men hate you, And when they exclude you, And revile you, and cast out your name as evil, For the Son of Man's sake. 23 Rejoice in that day and leap for joy! For indeed your reward is great in heaven, For in like manner their fathers did to the prophets.

> 24 "But woe to you who are rich, For you have received your consolation. 25 Woe to you who are full, For you shall hunger. Woe to you who laugh now, For you shall mourn and weep. 26 Woe to you when all men speak well of you, For so did their fathers to the false prophets.

Luke's version of the beatitudes is different from that of Matthew's account (Matthew 5:1-11) in several ways. One difference is that in Matthew Jesus addresses the crowd in third person - "Blessed are the poor in spirit," while in Luke, He addresses them in second person - "Blessed are you poor." The second difference is that Matthew adds "in spirit" to "poor," thus, "poor in spirit," while Luke does not (as is in the original texts). It simply says: "Blessed are you poor."

While it may be tempting to spiritualize this passage, the plain text says: Blessed are you – poor, who hunger now, who weep now, when men hate you, exclude you, and cast out your name as evil for the Son of Man's sake... [Why?] "For in like manner their fathers did to the prophets." The physical sufferings, social exclusion and mental anguish are compared with the prophets of old who suffered similarly. This message from Jesus in Luke's account seems endowed with the purpose of preparing His disciples for persecution for following Him.

Another difference from Matthew's account is that in Luke Jesus addresses the rich: "Woe to you who are rich..., full..., who laugh now..., when all men speak well of you, [why?] "For so did their fathers to the false prophets." The association is once again to prophets, but this time to false prophets who chose to please men rather than God for favor from men. False security and comfort will not last forever.

To those whose hearts wanted to hear more, Jesus continued with practical advice on how to respond when persecuted:

> 27 But I say to you who hear: Love your enemies, do good to those who hate you, 28 bless those who curse you, and pray for those who spitefully use you. 29 To him who strikes you on the one cheek, offer the other also. And from him who takes away your cloak, do not withhold your tunic either. 30 Give to everyone who asks of you. And from him who takes away your goods do not ask them back. 31 And just as you want men to do to you, you also do to them likewise."

> 35 But love your enemies, do good, and lend, hoping for nothing in return; and your reward will be great, and you will be sons of the Most High. For He is kind to the unthankful and evil. 36 Therefore be merciful, just as your Father also is merciful. 37 Judge not, and you shall not be judged. Condemn not, and you shall not be condemned. Forgive, and you will be forgiven. 38 *Give, and it will be given to you: good measure, pressed down, shaken together, and running over will be put into your bosom. For with the same measure that you use, it will be measured back to you.* (Italics added)

Verse 38 finishes the passage and serves as a summary, or a cap, on all that was said. What is one to give? It does not say money. The principle of being open-handed is taught, along with the principle of return. Whatever one gives will come back to him. The Amplified version of the Bible brings out this point a little better:

> 38 Give, and it will be given to you. They will pour into your lap a good measure—pressed down, shaken together, and running over [with no space left for more]. For with the standard of measurement you use [when you do good to others], it will be measured to you in return."

What can one give? One can give clothes and whatever the other is asking for (vss. 29-30,35). They can also give: love (vss. 27,35), goodness (vss. 27,35), blessings (vs. 28), prayer (vs. 28), mercy (vs. 36), no judgment (vs. 37), no condemnation (vs. 37), forgiveness (vs. 37), and whatever (vs. 38). The measure one uses is what is going to be measured back to them (vs. 38). "And just as you want men to do to you, you also do to them likewise" (vs. 31).

Who was to give? Jesus' disciples were. *To whom* were they to give? To the needy and to persecutors. *Why* were they to give? One reason was to manifest God's kingdom through His children. As the Father is merciful and kind to the unthankful (vss. 35-36) so should His children act the same. When they do, they will receive great heavenly rewards. They "will be sons of the Most High" (vs. 35). Besides the heavenly or spiritual rewards, earthly rewards awaited them as well: "it will be given to you: good measure, pressed down, shaken together, and running over will be put into your bosom" (vs. 38).

This passage so beautifully charges believers in Christ to be open handed to the needy, the undeserving, and even to their enemies. We might say that in this sermon Jesus described His own mission. He came to earth to a lowly, undeserving, faithless, selfish, proud, and

82

sinful people to raise them up out of their mire into new creations and into the heavenly realm. He came to love, give, and forgive unconditionally, and to extend mercy and grace to the undeserving. He prepared and urged His followers to treat each other the same. The heart of this message is not financial gain for doing good but extending grace and mercy to one another. No act of kindness will go on unnoticed and great rewards will await true followers of Christ.

The Pauline Discourse on Giving
2 Corinthians 8-9

Second Corinthians chapters eight and nine make up the longest discourse on giving in the New Testament. The background to the teaching is that the Apostle Paul made it one of his missions to collect funds for the poor Judean Christians in Jerusalem from the churches he visited. (According to church history, these Christians were poor due to persecution.) As such, he taught these churches about the "ins and outs" of giving. In his first letter to the Corinthian church, he instructed them on how to set aside their money contributions so they would be ready when he comes (1 Corinthians 16:1-4). In chapters 8 and 9 of 2 Corinthians he continues that theme, but primarily focusing on encouraging them to give generously.

Chapter eight begins with Paul's praise report about the Macedonian churches' sacrificial offerings for the poor. As the Macedonian churches gave "beyond their ability" (v. 3), Paul lets the Corinthian church know, in verses 5-8, that he recognizes the growing zeal to help the poor in them as well, and expresses this thought to them in verse 9:

> For you know the grace of our Lord Jesus Christ, that though He was rich, yet for your sakes He became poor, that you through His poverty might become rich.

This verse is repeatedly used in sermons to teach that it is God's will for us to become rich. However, the context of chapters 8-9 indicates differently. The point Paul is conveying is that giving introduces them

83

to an experiential knowledge of Christ's self-sacrificial spirit. As they give more of what they have to the needy by the grace of God, they identify with and become more acquainted with the Spirit of Christ, who gave until He became poor. Christ gave all His riches, Paul says, that they might be rich. The emphasis is on the *spirit of sacrificial giving*, not on the pursuit of becoming rich. This verse will be explored more deeply in a later chapter, under "Heavenly Riches."

In this sermon Paul offers two very important principles on giving under grace. They both pertain to *how much* to give. The first of these is found in 8:12-15:

> 12 ... if the [eager] readiness to give is there, then it is acceptable and welcomed in proportion to what a person has, not according to what he does not have. 13 For it is not [intended] that other people be eased and relieved [of their responsibility] and you be burdened and suffer [unfairly], 14 But to have *equality* [share and share alike], your surplus over necessity at the present time going to meet their want and to *equalize* the difference created by it, so that [at some other time] their surplus in turn may be given to supply your want. Thus, there may be *equality,* 15 As it is written, He who gathered much had nothing over, and he who gathered little did not lack. (2 Corinthians 8:12-15 Amp., italics added.)

Thus, the first principle is to give donations within their means so that they do not end up being in want. The goal is equality, and that no one lacks any basic necessities. Once this is understood, Paul then urges them, as a second principle, to sow abundantly, for God abundantly rewards those who give to the poor:

> 2 Corinthians 9:6 But this I say: He who sows sparingly will also reap sparingly, and he who sows bountifully will also reap bountifully. 7 So let each one give as he purposes in his heart, not grudgingly or of necessity; for God loves a cheerful giver. 8 And God is able to make all grace abound toward you, that you, always having all sufficiency

in all things, may have an abundance for every good work. 9 As it is written: "He has dispersed abroad, He has given to the poor; His righteousness endures forever."

Some people may be surprised to read in this passage that Paul is talking about sowing into the poor. In the countless sermons I heard on this passage, the reading of the Word stopped at the end of verse seven or eight. Verse nine was consistently left off, likely because of the belief that sowing into to the poor was not a good investment. But then the sermon would continue with verse ten to the end of the chapter:

> 10 Now he who supplies seed to the sower and bread for food will also supply and increase your store of seed and will enlarge the harvest of your righteousness. 11 You will be enriched in every way so that you can be generous on every occasion, and through us your generosity will result in thanksgiving to God.

> 12 This service that you perform is not only supplying the needs of the Lord's people but is also overflowing in many expressions of thanks to God. 13 Because of the service by which you have proved yourselves, others will praise God for the obedience that accompanies your confession of the gospel of Christ, and for your generosity in sharing with them and with everyone else. 14 And in their prayers for you their hearts will go out to you, because of the surpassing grace God has given you. 15 Thanks be to God for his indescribable gift!

Leaving verse nine out, the promises of verses 6-15 are misrepresented, which are the promises that follow giving to the poor and not to other recipients. Verses 6-7 are very commonly taught from pulpits for their promises of reaping for sowing, like Luke 6:38. But in each of these cases, the promises follow sowing into the poor. When the focus becomes on reaping riches, instead of teaching sowing into the poor, the exact opposite is delivered from the pulpit – that of sowing into the "blessed," or rich, believing it to be better soil.

How we give greatly matters to God in these passages. One should give out of the heart: cheerfully, and not grudgingly, reluctantly, sorrowfully or under compulsion (verses 6-7). The *reasons to give* are:

1. to help the needy in their affliction (9:12)
2. to attain equality in the body of Christ (8:12-15)
3. the giver receives immense blessings:
    – reaps generously (9:6)
    – God's grace abounds toward him (9:8)
    – always has all sufficiency in all things (9:8)
    – has an abundance for every good work (9:8)
    – his righteousness endures forever (9:9)
4. giving brings forth thanksgiving to God (9:11-12)
5. the receivers glorify God for the givers' obedience and liberality and yearn and pray for the givers because of the grace of God in them. (9:14)

In conclusion, the recipients in these two chapters are the poor, specifically, poor *believers* (of the household of faith), and the purpose for giving is to meet their needs. Giving to the poor is giving to God. Giving to God always results in blessings and rewards. We can bring nothing to God that He does not bless and reward. This is a sure promise. But not only those who give are blessed, but also those who receive, as this passage so beautifully points out.

Worthy of notice in this discourse, as in the previous passages, that no mention of tenth or any given amount is named, only guidelines and appeals to give. This is very significant. If tithing was to continue by believers in Christ, this passage would be the one most likely to include teaching on tithing, since it is addressed to gentiles not accustomed to tithing. Yet there is no reference to any tithe, or to any specific amount to give. Giving is not governed by an outside force, such as a code of law, but from the heart for the Christian on whose heart the law of God is written. Out of the heart they give.

Galatians 6:7
Context: Galatians 6:6-10

> 6 Let him who is taught the word share in all good
> things with him who teaches. *7 Do not be deceived,*
> *God is not mocked; for whatever a man sows, that he*
> *will also reap.* 8 For he who sows to his flesh will of
> the flesh reap corruption, but he who sows to the Spirit
> will of the Spirit reap everlasting life. 9 And let us not
> grow weary while doing good, for in due season we
> shall reap if we do not lose heart. 10 Therefore, as we
> have opportunity, let us do good to all, especially to
> those who are of the household of faith. (Italics added)

Galatians 6:7, particularly the second half of the verse, "for whatever a
man sows, that he will also reap" is a very commonly quoted principle.
From this comes the teaching, that if we sow money, we reap money.
Testimonies have been given of people giving a watch and reaped many
watches, or giving a ring, and reaped many rings, etc. More in line with
Scripture, sowing is also associated with seed growing in soil – that a
particular seed produces after its own kind, not another. Now, the seed
contains life in itself and is designed to grow, but what do inanimate
objects have that make them grow?

What leaps out from verse seven is the warning: "Do not be deceived,
God is not mocked..." It may seem odd to include this thought with
sowing and reaping. The warning implies the heart, and the motive of
the heart. The next verse mentions two soils to sow into: the flesh or
the Spirit. True life is only found in the Spirit, and sowing to the Spirit
reaps everlasting life. Sowing to anything else than the life-giving
Spirit, such as to the flesh, reaps only corruption, the verse says.

If we return to verse 6, we find instruction to those taught the Word to
"share in all good things with him who teaches." Sharing of good things
could mean partnering with, or "contributing to his support" (AMP).
Since teaching the Word is sowing the Word, contributing to the person

sowing the Word is comparable to sowing to the Spirit, Who gives eternal life.

God cares about our hearts. He wants us to make good decisions with our resources. So, Paul continues: "let us not grow weary while doing good, for in due season we shall reap..." Thus, reaping is associated with doing good works. The passage does not mention money, and the focus is on the heart from which we give "whatsoever," which should produce eternal life.

This passage brings to attention a new target group to support: teachers of the Word. 1Timothy 5:17-18 echoes the same:

> 17 The elders who perform their leadership duties well are to be considered worthy of double honor (financial support), especially those who work hard at preaching and teaching [the word of God concerning eternal salvation through Christ]. (AMP)
> 18 For the Scripture says, "You shall not muzzle an ox while it treads out the grain," and, "The laborer is worthy of his wages." (NKJV)

When Paul wrote this letter, ministers of the Gospel were likely not on salaried positions. Paul was teaching his young converts in several different letters about their responsibility and duty to support those who labor among them. At this point we make mention of the fact that the New Testament always instructs to give either to the poor or to those who serve the Lord – apostles, teachers, evangelists, missionaries, etc. These match the same two groups of people as for the tithe. The last passage on giving is another one about supporting God's servant: Paul, the evangelist/missionary.

Philippians 4:19
"And my God shall supply all your need according to
His riches in glory by Christ Jesus."

A church that understood the concept of supporting those who labor among them, and contributed to Paul's ministry, was the church at Philippi:

> 14 But it was right and commendable and noble of you to contribute for my needs and to share my difficulties with me. (Amp) 15 Now you Philippians know also that in the beginning of the gospel, when I departed from Macedonia, no church shared with me concerning giving and receiving but you only. 16 For even in Thessalonica you sent aid once and again for my necessities. 17 Not that I seek the gift, but I seek the fruit that abounds to your account. 18 Indeed I have all and abound. I am full, having received from Epaphroditus the things sent from you, a sweet-smelling aroma, an acceptable sacrifice, well pleasing to God. 19 And my God shall supply all your need according to His riches in glory by Christ Jesus. (Philippians 4:15-19)

The recipient was the Apostle Paul. The purposes for sowing were manyfold. Sowing involved contributing to Paul's needs and sharing his difficulties with him (vs 14). The gifts did not only meet his needs, encouraged, and blessed him, but also bore fruit to their account (vs 17). What does "fruit to their account" mean? One explanation I have heard is that the "account" is like a bank account in heaven from which one can draw money through giving. So, giving increases one's account in heaven, and multiplies one's seed here on earth.

The Greek word translated as "account," is, interestingly, "*logos*." *Logos* is most commonly translated as "word." Examples where *logos* is translated as "account" are: "But I say to you that for every idle word men may speak, they will give account (*logos*) of it in the day of judgment" (Matthew 12:36), "So then each of us shall give account (*logos*) of himself to God" (Romans 14:12.) What we do and say counts and we will have to report it in the day of judgment. Either we are "being filled with fruits of righteousness which are by Jesus Christ, to the glory and praise of God," (Philippians 1:11), or are engaging in works that do not count for eternity:

> 12 Now if anyone builds on this foundation with gold, silver, precious stones, wood, hay, straw, 13 each one's work will become clear; for the Day will declare it, because it will be revealed by fire; and the fire will test each one's work, of what sort it is. 14 If anyone's work which he has built on it endures, he will receive a reward. 15 If anyone's work is burned, he will suffer loss; but he himself will be saved, yet so as through fire. (1 Corinthians 3:12-15)

So, when Paul says, "Not that I seek the gift, but I seek the fruit that abounds to your account" he means that by supporting him he is happy that they increase their heavenly rewards.

What does "my God shall supply all your need *according to His riches in glory by Christ Jesus*" mean? The word "riches," in the phrase "riches in glory," pertains to *His glory*. Unger's Bible Dictionary defines Glory as: "Glory is the expression of holiness," and, "... the manifestation of His divine attributes and perfections..." Baker Encyclopedia of the Bible states: Glory is "the singular splendor of God and its consequences for mankind."

Glory refers to all that God is. Glory describes the splendor, majesty, and praiseworthiness of God. How does one describe the extent of God's glory? Rich? God is rich in glory – in splendor, majesty, and praiseworthiness. The richness or riches of His glory – who He is – we experience *by* Christ Jesus, or, as other translations say, *in* Christ Jesus. So, we read: "...according to His riches in glory by Christ Jesus." Thus, by-, in-, through Christ Jesus, God will supply (what?) "all your *need*." Paul is not saying that God will supply them with riches or wealth above their needs, but that *all* their needs will be met. The Amplified version explains the verse this way: "And my God will liberally supply (fill until full) *your every need* according to His riches in glory in Christ Jesus" (italics added).

There is no demand from Paul for any offering or support, just joy expressed for the fruit that will abound to their account for supporting him. Giving is personal. All aspects of giving, that of what, when, how much, how often, etc. are born out of the Holy Spirit's leading and of their hearts' desires.

Common Theme

A common theme in the above passages is that giving to the poor and to those who are called to full time spiritual service is pleasing to the Lord, and great rewards await those who give. The two categories of people are the same as in the biblical tithe, and reflective of the rest of the New Testament, for one finds no other group of people to give to. Taking care of the poor and of His servants always was and always will be in the heart of God.

From a different perspective, a common theme in the above passages is the inclusion of the sowing and reaping principle. These are choice Scriptures in prosperity teaching to encourage people to give. Giving should never be discouraged, but it must line up with the Word of God. One must ask, "Who is the money going to?" and, "For what purpose?" These questions are important in light of the promises of reaping for sowing. Only sowing into the people specified do the Scriptures guarantee reaping.

Sowing and reaping are agricultural terms, referring to a farmer sowing his seed in the field and reaping his harvest at the end of the growing season. Combining this analogy with the verse that "whatever a man sows, that he will also reap," an interpretation is heard that if a man sows money he will bring in a harvest of money. The scriptural basis

91

for this interpretation is the parable of the sower and the seed. Can this deduction be made from this passage?

The Parable of the Sower and the Seed
Mark 4:1-20

3 Give attention to this!" (*Amp*) "Listen!" (*Other versions*). Behold, a sower went out to sow. 4 And it happened, as he sowed, that some seed fell by the wayside; and the birds of the air came and devoured it. 5 Some fell on stony ground, where it did not have much earth; and immediately it sprang up because it had no depth of earth. 6 But when the sun was up it was scorched, and because it had no root it withered away. 7 And some seed fell among thorns; and the thorns grew up and choked it, and it yielded no crop. 8 But other seed fell on good ground and yielded a crop that sprang up, increased and produced: some thirtyfold, some sixty, and some a hundred." 9 And He said to them, "He who has ears to hear, let him hear!" (NKJV) 9 He said, He who has ears to hear, let him be hearing [and let him consider, and comprehend]" (Amp)

The disciples attentively listened, along with the huge crowd, but had no clue what Jesus was talking about. When they were able to get Jesus alone, they asked Him to explain what He meant.

And He said to them, Do you not discern and understand this parable? How then is it possible for you to discern and understand all the parables? (v. 13, Amp)

There was something special about this parable they had to get. The explanation turned out to be rather plain and simple. "The sower sows the Word" (vs 14). The seed is the Word of God that is planted in hearts likened to different soils (verses 15-20). If you do not get this word, Jesus might say, nothing else will make sense.

This parable is not so much about sowing, but about *receiving* (the Word). It is not about the sower, but about the seed and the soil. And, it is not about a reaper, but about bearing fruit. These distinctions are significant. When the principle of sowing and reaping is taught, the central focus is on the sower, who is also the reaper of the harvest. But this parable does not mention any reaper. The emphasis is on the fruit. What is the fruit?

First, one has to recognize that the fruit is not the seed. The fruit *contains* the seed. The seed simply does not multiply itself like a single cell organism that multiplies by division, and never changes. The seed *becomes* a plant first, and then bears seed-containing fruit. In case of a fruit tree, for example, first the seed grows into a beautiful, flowering tree, then it produces juicy, tasty fruits that carry the seeds. How does this compare with the Word of God sown in our hearts? The seed of the Word is sown with the Holy Spirit. Through the agency of the Holy Spirit the seed grows into a beautiful life, representing the attributes of God: love, joy, peace, patience, kindness, goodness, faithfulness, gentleness and self-control (Galatians 5:22-23). These attributes are called the *fruit of the Spirit.* Since the seed is eternal, the seed also bears another fruit: eternal life.

What does "thirty, sixty, and a hundredfold" mean? The dictionary defines "hundredfold" as "a hundred times as great or as much." Therefore, we can surmise, that "thirty, sixty, and a hundredfold" means both, spiritual growth and multiplication. A ripe fruit not only contains seeds, but it is ready to release them into new soil. Saved souls are, doubtless, part of fruit bearing. This concept is quite contrary to the message taught that one is to sow in order to reap more *for themselves*.

The seed can only grow and flourish in the right environment and under favorable conditions. The same is true for the Word of God. The Scriptures tell us that the Word is *alive* (Hebrews 4:12) and that it is Jesus (John 1:1-3, 14). When the seed of the Word is sown into our hearts, it needs a favorable environment. It needs to be protected and nurtured. This parable points out those things that hinder God's Word from growing in our hearts, and also shows what enables God's Word to grow.

One hindrance is a heart that is like stony ground. Even though a person hears the word and gladly receives it, the root in that stony ground (hard heart) cannot grow deep, and when persecution arises, they are too weak to stand, and end up falling away (verses 16-17). Others may hear the Word, but "the cares of this world, the deceitfulness of riches, and the desires for other things entering in choke the Word, and it becomes unfruitful" (verses 18-19). In other words, there is no place for Christ to grow in these hearts. Other things take precedence in time and rulership. Christ cannot become the Lord in these peoples' lives. Getting rid of those distractions would be required for growth to occur. The best soil, according to Jesus, are hearts that "hear the word, accept it, and bear fruit: some thirty-fold, some sixty, and some a hundred" (vs 20). Christ, the Word, is welcomed in these hearts, and allowed to grow and rule.

Can money grow and reproduce the same way a seed can? According to the prosperity gospel, yes. Investing money into the kingdom is taught to reap a thirty, sixty, and a hundred-fold depending on the "soil" the money is sown into. With no more effort, other than, perhaps, "calling it in," the money is presumed to reproduce itself even while we sleep, as some teach from Mark 4:26-29:

> 26 And He said, "The kingdom of God is as if a man should scatter seed on the ground, 27 and should sleep by night and rise by day, and the seed should sprout and grow, he himself does not know how. 28 For the earth yields crops by itself: first the blade, then the head, after that the full grain in the head. 29 But when the grain ripens, immediately he puts in the sickle, because the harvest has come."

Neither the subject matter (the kingdom of God) nor the illustration (the seed and crop) in this passage has to do with money. But it is taught that money grows like plants and can produce the same way and at the same rate: thirty, sixty, and a hundred-fold. If this would be true, one should fully expect a harvest of $3,000 on every $100 sown at a "low" rate of thirty-fold return. A rate of a thirty-fold return would be splendid if it were true, and no one would work a day in their life! A hundred-fold increase would bring in $10,000 on every $100 sown!

In both of the above parables, the point is not on multiplication of the seed itself: thirty, sixty, and a hundred-fold, but on fruit bearing. In good soil the seed turns into fruit and that is what is harvested. The goal is: bearing fruit. What fruit is produced from sowing money? If it is sown into healthy ministries, it should bear fruit for the kingdom: people getting saved, healed, delivered, and growing in the Lord. This is the kind of fruit bearing that money could produce, and not money multiplied back to self. This is not to say that God cannot bless us with more money as we give. But that is not implicated in these parables. Rather, they confirm the Scripture previously discussed in Philippians 4:17: "Not that I seek the gift, but I seek the *fruit* that abounds to your account." That is, *heavenly rewards* wait for those who give and sacrifice.

The truth is, one loses sight of spiritual fruit bearing when reaping money on money sown is taught. If one's heart is given to reaping money, his focus will be on *money*: on watching, waiting, "nurturing it" with confessions, calling it in, etc. This preoccupation with money may be the very thing that could choke the Word in one's heart: "the cares of this world, the deceitfulness of riches, and the desires for other things entering in choke the Word, and it becomes unfruitful."

Is this parable taught in a way that actually contradicts the very message Jesus intended to convey? One wonders how many people truly know and understand the *real* meaning of this parable and its important principle.

HEAVENLY VS EARTHLY REWARDS

The New Testament mentions both earthly and heavenly rewards. The earthly rewards are promised in the form of meeting all our needs – abundantly. In Luke 6:38 Jesus promises a return on giving to overflowing and running over, and in 2 Corinthians 9:8 Paul promises "all sufficiency in all things, (that you) may have an abundance for every good work." In Philippians 4:19 Paul asserts that God shall supply *all* their needs. Meeting all our needs is big on God's agenda. Lack is never on His agenda for us. These promises follow helping the poor and needy. The Apostle Paul was needy from the perspective that He relied on God's provision to carry out his ministry. But heavenly rewards are also sure to follow those who give to the poor, as Paul stated in Philippians and as Jesus taught:

> Luke 12:33 "Sell what you possess and give donations to the poor; provide yourselves with purses and handbags that do not grow old, an unfailing and inexhaustible *treasure in the heavens*, where no thief comes near and no moth destroys. 34 For where your treasure is, there your heart will be also." (AMP, italics added)

> Luke 18:22 "When Jesus heard this, he said to him, "You still lack one thing. Sell everything you have and give to the poor, and you will have *treasure in heaven*. Then come, follow me." (NIV, italics added)

> Matthew 6:19 "Do not store up for yourselves [material] treasures on earth, where moth and rust destroy, and where thieves break in and steal. 20 But store up for yourselves *treasures in heaven*, where neither moth nor rust destroys, and where thieves do not break in and steal; 21 for where your treasure is, there your heart [your wishes, your desires; that on which your life centers] will be also." (AMP, italics added)

How literally Jesus meant these things is debatable, but Jesus is pointing out that giving to the poor brings rewards, and these rewards are not earthly (more money), but heavenly (treasures in heaven). So, when we have sown and sown and see no harvest of money, perhaps it is because the reward is awarded to us in heaven. Jesus' words actually warn against storing treasures on earth. But the heart of His teaching is not so much about money or possessions, but on the heart of man – that tends to follow his money. So, where we sow our money is of great significance. In this instance, giving to the poor strikes a chord with God – where His heart is – and earns us treasures I heaven.

Could one exchange heavenly rewards for earthly? This statement by Jesus suggests so: "So when you give to the needy, do not announce it with trumpets, as the hypocrites do in the synagogues and on the streets, to be honored by others. Truly I tell you, they have received their reward in full." (Matthew 6:2) Thus, the reward was received on earth from men and no reward was left for heaven. Interestingly, there is no mention of *more money* as a reward. The earthly reward is simply the recognition they get from men.

The prosperity teaching presented in this book clearly focuses on earthly rewards – riches here on earth. As we saw, rewards are guaranteed in the Word of God but not necessarily here on earth. Is the expectation of 30-60-100-fold financial return, deducted from the parable of the sower and the seed, realistic and biblical? When living in such expectation, are we able to heed the Scriptures on being content with what we have?

> 5 Let your conduct be without covetousness; be content
> with such things as you have. For He Himself has said, "I
> will never leave you nor forsake you." (Hebrews 13:5-6)

The Amplified version (Classic Edition) of the same text expresses so beautifully God's amazing hold on us – that we don't need to worry about our provision:

5 Let your character or moral disposition be free from love of money [including greed, avarice, lust, and craving for earthly possessions] and be satisfied with your present [circumstances and with what you have]; for He [God] Himself has said, I will not in any way fail you nor give you up nor leave you without support. [I will] not, [I will] not, [I will] not in any degree leave you helpless nor forsake nor let [you] down (relax My hold on you)! [Assuredly not!] (AMPC)

Paul's advice to Timothy is in the same vein:

6 Now godliness with contentment is great gain. 7 For we brought nothing into this world, and it is certain we can carry nothing out. 8 And having food and clothing, with these we shall be content. (1 Timothy 6:6-8)

17 Command those who are rich in this present age not to be haughty, nor to trust in uncertain riches but in the living God, who gives us richly all things to enjoy. 18 Let them do good, that they be rich in good works, ready to give, willing to share, 19 storing up for themselves a good foundation for the time to come, that they may lay hold on eternal life. (1 Timothy 6:17-19)

If giving to the poor earns heavenly rewards, what should our response be? Should we not pursue riches so we can give more? How do we pursue riches? Are we all to be wealthy? PART III leads into a discussion on riches and wealth in God's Word.

PART III: PROSPERITY, WEALTH AND RICHES

PROSPERITY: NEW TESTAMENT

3 John 2
Beloved, I pray that you may prosper in all things and
be in health, just as your soul prospers.

This heartfelt greeting from Paul to his beloved friend, Gaius, has become one of the most quoted Scripture on prosperity. This verse has become the cornerstone, if not the only Scripture, the prosperity doctrine is built on, much like Malachi 3:8-10 is the cornerstone and almost only Scripture the tithing doctrine is built on. Undoubtedly, this verse reveals God's agenda for us to prosper. However, as with the term "tithe" that has a biblical meaning which is different from the meaning attached to it today, the term "prosperity" has a biblical meaning which is different from the meaning commonly attached to it today, namely, financial prosperity and wealth.

In this verse and in this translation (NKJV) the Greek word that is translated "prosper" is "*euodoo*" (*Strong's*, #2137*)* and is defined as: "to help on the road," "succeed in reaching," "to succeed in business affairs," and, "(have) a prosperous journey." Since none of these meanings say "prosper" per se, one might ask if other translations of the Bible opt for "prosper" in this verse.   Here are some examples (translation of *euodoo* is in italics):

Greek/English Interlinear Bible: "Beloved, in regard to all things, I pray (for) you *to do well*, and to be in health, as your soul does well."
NIV: "Dear friend, I pray that you may enjoy good health and that *all may go well with you*, even as your soul is getting along well."
MSG: "I pray for good fortune in everything you do, and for your good health—that *your everyday affairs prosper*, as well as your soul!
NASB: "I pray that *in all respects you may prosper...*,"
Amplified: "I pray that *you may prosper in every way....*"

99

This Greek word *euodoo* occurs only two other times in the New Testament: Romans 1:10 and 1 Corinthians 16:2. The context and various translations shed further light on the meaning of this word. Here are some examples:

Romans 1:10 (in four translations):
Amplified: "...by God's will I may now at last *prosper* and come to you."
KJV: "...I might *have a prosperous journey* by the will of God to come unto you"
NASB: "...perhaps now at last by the will of God *I may succeed* in coming to you"
MSG: "...I ask him *to clear the way* for me to come and see you"

The word expresses success for a desired trip. It has nothing to do with material wealth in this verse.

1 Corinthians 16:2 (in three translations):
Amplified: "On the first [day] of each week, let each one of you [personally] put aside something and save it up *as he has prospered* [in proportion to what he is given], so that no collections will need to be taken after I come."
NIV: "On the first day of every week, each one of you should set aside a sum of money *in keeping with your income*, saving it up, so that when I come no collections will have to be made:"
MSG: "Every Sunday each of you make an offering and put it in safekeeping. Be as generous as you can. When I get there you'll have it ready, and I won't have to make a special appeal."

As one can see, the closest synonym of prosper is "succeed" and it can apply to any and all areas of life. John wishes in 3 John 2 that his friend, Gaius, "may prosper in all things." "All things" could mean work, ministry, family, relationships, business, finances, and even one's soul! How could one's soul prosper? If we consider that the soul is made up of mind, will, and emotions, we could say that the soul may prosper in

100

mind – growing (succeeding) in knowledge, understanding, and wisdom; in will – making sound decisions, obeying the Lord, choosing to forgive others; and, in emotions – feeling/experiencing peace, joy, and love.

Going well with, or prospering in every way, certainly includes finances, but to reduce the word to mean *only* finances misuses and misrepresents God's Word. Knowing the correct meaning of the word is critical for proper interpretation of other verses where the translators opt for the word "prosper" or "prosperity." Let us see how this proves to be true for Old Testament Scriptures on prosperity.

PROSPERITY: OLD TESTAMENT

Psalm 35:27 is sort of an Old Testament equivalent of 3 John 2, in that it is often quoted to show that it is God's will and desire for us all to be financially wealthy:

> Let them shout for joy and be glad, Who favor my righteous cause; And let them say continually, "Let the Lord be magnified, Who has pleasure in the *prosperity* of His servant." (Italics added)

This verse is frequently heard in tithing sermons to help us get the point that it is God's great desire for us to become rich. Is that what the translator intended to mean when he chose the English word "prosperity?" The Hebrew word translated "prosperity" in this verse is "*shalom*"! *Shalom* is most often translated as "peace" in the Bible and only a handful of times it is translated as "prosperity" or "prosperous." The word conveys a broad meaning – things that pertain to and bring about peace. *Strong's Exhaustive Concordance* uses the following words to describe "*Shalom*" (#7965): "safe - well, happy, friendly; welfare – health, prosperity, peace." It is noteworthy that neither "wealthy" or "rich" is part of the list, and no English translation uses either of these words. No doubt, financial success is included in the term, but "*shalom*" covers the whole spectrum of life. To equate "*shalom*" (Hebrew) and "prosperity" (English) with wealth and riches only, is to misrepresent God's Word. How do other translations represent "*shalom*" in this verse? Here are some examples:

"...Great is the Lord, who delights in the *welfare* of his servant!" (RSV)
"...Jehovah is magnified, Who is desiring the *peace* of His servant." (Young's Literal Translation)
"...The Lord be exalted, who delights in the *well-being* of his servant." (NIV)

A cousin word to "*shalom*" is "*shalah*" (#7951), which is also sometimes translated as "prosper." *Strong's* interpretation of this Hebrew word is: "to be tranquil, i.e., secure or successful: - be happy, prosper, be in safety. This word is found in Psalm 122:6: "Pray for the peace of Jerusalem: they shall prosper that love thee." If we interpret prosper to mean mere wealth, we miss the rich promises of God that those who love and pray for Jerusalem will also be tranquil, secure, successful, happy and safe. Quite a difference!

We have seen how "*shalom*" can be translated, and that it is sometimes translated as "prosper." Are there other Hebrew words that get the English equivalent "prosper?" Here are two common ones:

1. "Tsalach" [6743]: break out, come (mightily), go over, be good, be profitable, cause to...prosper.
2. "Sakal" [7919]: to be circumspect and hence intelligent: consider, expert, instruct, prosper, prudent, skillful, have good success, understand(ing), wisdom, wise, guide wittingly.

Scriptures where these words appear are:

Psalm 1:3 He shall be like a tree planted by the rivers of water, that brings forth its fruit in its season, whose leaf also shall not wither; And whatever he does shall *prosper* [Tsalach, 6743]. (NKJV)

Joshua 1:7 Only be strong and very courageous, that you may observe to do according to all the law which Moses My servant commanded you; do not turn from it to the right hand or to the left, that you may *prosper* [Sakal, 7919] wherever you go. 8 This Book of the Law shall not depart from your mouth, but you shall meditate in it day and night, that you may observe to do according to all that is written in it. For then you will make your way *prosperous* [Tsalach, 6743], and then you will have good *success* [Sakal, 7919]

Neither "wealthy" or "rich" would make good translations in any of these verses. These examples well reflect the meaning of biblical prosperity. Whether Greek or Hebrew, the original words that are translated as "prosper" or "prosperity," all indicate ongoing success on life's journey in every area of life through a close walk with the Lord. In that place He always blesses in spirit, soul, body, and in all affairs of life. This meaning comes across in every verse that talks about prosperity in the Bible. Equating prosperity with just wealth and riches is misrepresenting God's Word.

How did we arrive at mere "wealth and riches" for "prosperity" in our sermons? The dictionary definition does reflect the other meanings -- that of success in every area of life. The almost exclusive usage of wealth and riches is not surprising in today's culture where the attainment of material/financial success seems paramount to all other endeavors, and where prosperity has come to mean primarily financial success. In many sermons, prosperity has become synonymous with material blessings, or wealth and riches, as we subtly engage in a war against a "poverty mentality" in our churches. Could our focus have quietly shifted from morality, integrity, strength of character and spiritual maturity to personal gain and financial success, like the world has? While receiving God's blessings for our material needs, are we

103

shifting our goals on attaining more of the blessings than more of God? Are we sowing only to get more? Biblical prosperity is a *consequence*, or a result, of following biblical principles, and it entails every area of life. It can hardly be pursued on its own. Yet some prosperity teaching has made it a goal and a pursuit.

HOW BIBLICAL PROSPERITY IS ATTAINED

Perhaps the clearest way to see the difference between biblical prosperity and the prosperity concept this book addresses is by observing how they are attained. The prosperity teaching instructs us to sow for it. The Bible teaches something quite different.

3 John 2, as we saw, clearly connects life-prosperity with soul-prosperity. Some examples of what soul-prosperity might look like were given. Other ways to attain biblical prosperity can be derived by:
  – favoring God's righteous cause (Psalm 35:27)
  – praying for the peace of Jerusalem; loving Jerusalem (Psalm 122:6)
  – not walking in the counsel of the ungodly (Psalm 1:1)
  – not standing in the path of sinners (Psalm 1:1)
  – not sitting in the seat of the scornful (Psalm 1:1)
  – delighting in the law of the Lord (Psalm 1:2)
  – meditating in His law day and night (Psalm 1:2)

Perhaps the best summary to the path of prosperity is Joshua 1:8:

> This Book of the Law shall not depart from your mouth, but you shall meditate in it day and night, that you may observe to do according to all that is written in it. For then you will make your way prosperous, and then you will have good success.

As we see, the conditions for attaining biblical prosperity according to these verses are drastically different from the idea of sowing money for it. And here lies the core difference between the meanings. One is a *consequence* of good choices and is characterized primarily by soul prosperity. The other is a direct *pursuit* of wealth and riches.

Are we instructed to pursue riches in the Bible? Based on the previous Scriptures and Matthew 6:33 the answer seems to be simple. Prosperity – financial and other – are blessings of the Lord and we are to pursue Him and His righteousness, and "all these things shall be added unto us" (Matthew 6:33).

WEALTH AND RICHES IN GOD'S WORD

New Covenant Brings New Perspective

Wealth and riches seem to be viewed quite differently in the two covenants – the Old and the New. Under the Old Covenant wealth and riches represented God's presence with the Jewish nation. God gave them a vast land – the most valuable of all commodities – and the spoil of the land. Then He caused wealth to transfer to them from other nations, as we see in the case of Abraham, Solomon, and others. God lavished the nation with wealth, and reminded them that it was by *His* hand and not by their own works:

> And you shall remember the Lord your God, for it is He who gives you power to get wealth, that He may establish His covenant which He swore to your fathers, as it is this day. (Deuteronomy 8:18)

Being wealthy was a covenant matter. As long as they feared God, one of His many blessings was wealth and riches:

> Praise the Lord! Blessed is the man who fears the Lord, Who delights greatly in His commandments. His descendants will be mighty on earth;
> The generation of the upright will be blessed. Wealth and riches will be in his house, And his righteousness endures forever. (Psalm 112:1-3)

However, warnings abounded about the snares of and trusting in riches rather than in God. It does not belong to the wicked or unrighteous. No doubt that in the right relationship with God He wanted His choice nation to be the richest on earth.

As we turn to the New Testament, we see a clear shift in perspective. The Old Testament is primarily about receiving (land, riches, etc.), while the New Testament is about giving. In the Old Testament, God, with whom the people had only a distant relationship, required just ten percent of what they freely received to be given back to Him. In the New Testament, the believers are challenged to give it all, as modeled by Christ. When John the Baptist met up with the Pharisees and Sadducees, they might have thought it a radical idea to share half of some of their goods with the poor, when John so instructed them. The rich young ruler may have been profoundly shocked at hearing such an unconventional or even bizarre suggestion as to give away *all* his possessions to the poor. The disciples may have taken a big gulp when Jesus told them to:

> Sell what you have and give alms; provide yourselves money bags which do not grow old, a treasure in the heavens that does not fail, where no thief approaches nor moth destroys. For where your treasure is, there your heart will be also. (Luke 12:33-34)

Jesus inaugurated a New Covenant, and with it a new system of living, a new *focus* on life – one that is away from self and unto others. The focus is not only on one's own prosperity any more, but on helping bring prosperity to others: "...look out not only for his (one's) own interests, but also for the interests of others" (Philippians 2:4); encourage one another in the Lord (Hebrews 10:25); build up one another (Ephesians 4:12); help the poor (Luke 12:33); and "go into all the world and preach the gospel to all creation"(Mark 16:15). The focus of Jesus was to bring us "spiritual prosperity" – that we may all find the Father and be born into His family. He exemplified selflessness and

106

"other-centeredness," when he left His glorious, peaceful, exulted place in Heaven and came to us to give us His life. He gave up *everything* He could. As His disciples, we are to walk in His footsteps.

As we see, Jesus' teachings don't match the mindset of the Old Testament. How do we respond to such a change in perspective? How do we believe? How do wealth and riches fit into this? Doesn't God want us to be financially successful and be wise with our money in order to gain more? Isn't that what He intended to teach by the parable of the talents (Matthew 25:14-30)?

Reading the account of the New Testament, one finds that Jesus did not speak favorably about the rich or having riches. Neither did the other authors of the New Testament. Of the over 30 references to earthly riches, all are unfavorable, except a couple that are "neutral" - neither favorable nor unfavorable. How could this be?

One reason for this, I believe, is that Jesus came to deliver us all from spiritual bondage and oppression. Since oppression of the poor was prevalent of His day, primarily at the hands of the rich, much sympathy is expressed toward the poor, and disfavor, and even judgment toward the rich. The book of James, particularly, addresses some of the sentiments of Jesus toward these two societal groups. Most of the Scriptures on sowing/giving are directives to give to the poor. These were not lazy, but severely oppressed people.

Another reason, I believe, why wealth and riches are presented in unfavorable light in the New Testament, is that riches strongly contend and vie for the hearts of men.

> 23 Then Jesus looked around and said to His disciples, "How hard it is for those who have riches to enter the kingdom of God!" 24 And the disciples were astonished at His words. But Jesus answered again and said to them, "Children, how hard it is for those who trust in

riches to enter the kingdom of God! 25 It is easier for a
camel to go through the eye of a needle than for a rich
man to enter the kingdom of God." (Mark 10:23-25)

It is entering the kingdom of God that is at stake. Wealth definitely has
a way to lure people to pursue it and to base their security in it. Riches,
per se, are not the problem, but the pursuit of them without God, and
trusting in them, are. "Those who desire to be rich fall into temptation
and a snare..." (1 Timothy 6:9). Since the kingdom of God is a spiritual
kingdom reigning in men's hearts (until Jesus sets up His kingdom on
earth), both, riches and Jesus vie for the hearts of men. But there is only
room for one. Jesus said it this way: "No one can serve two masters;
for either he will hate the one and love the other, or he will be devoted
to the one and despise the other. You cannot serve God and mammon."
(Matthew 6:24)

While it is very hard for a rich man to enter the kingdom of God,
according to Jesus, He continued His sermon to say, that "with God all
things are possible (Mark 10:27). He certainly can change hearts, and
without God, really, *no one* could be saved: "Who then can be saved?"
asked the disciples, "But looking at them, Jesus said, "With men it is
impossible but not with God...." A rich person can be humble and not
serve mammon, while a poor can be covetous and hungry for riches.
The condition of the heart is what is expressed in the Beatitudes
according to Matthew: "Blessed are the poor *in spirit* for theirs is the
kingdom of heaven (Matthew 5:3). Poverty or lack is what creates
hunger.

Because the poor are most impoverished (whether physical or
spiritual), the poor are hailed as the best candidates to receive the
kingdom into their hearts, according to the Gospels. There is no
temptation to be fought, unlike for the wealthy to trust in their riches.
Thus, we read: "Blessed are you poor, For yours is the kingdom of
God." (Luke 6:20).

Heavenly Riches

> Listen, my beloved brethren: Has not God chosen those who are poor in the eyes of the world to be rich in faith and in their position as believers and to inherit the kingdom which He has promised to those who love Him? (James 2:5)

Hearing the word "rich," most people think of material wealth. The above verse takes that thinking to another level of understanding riches. Earthly poverty is contrasted with being "rich in faith," which is equated with loving God. One learns that kingdom wealth is not necessarily earthly wealth. The meaning of "rich" is greatly expanded under the New Covenant. Understanding this is foundational to interpreting many of the verses in the New Testament.

Dictionary.com lists 19 different uses of "rich," and only three of those refer to material possessions. The Bible adds to that list, as the focus of the New Testament diverts from earthly things to heavenly things, and from earthly riches to heavenly riches. Here are some ways the Bible uses riches:

- "Oh, the depth of the riches both of the wisdom and knowledge of God!" (Romans 11:33)
- "riches of their liberality" (2 Cor 8:2)
- "riches of His grace" (Ephesians 1:7)
- "riches of the glory of his inheritance" (Ephesians 1:18)
- "unsearchable riches of Christ" (Ephesians 3:8)
- "(Moses) considering the reproach of Christ greater riches than the treasures of Egypt" (Hebrews 11:26)
- "let the word of Christ dwell in you richly" (Colossians 3:16)
- "who gives us richly all things to enjoy" (1 Timothy 6:17)
- "God being rich in mercy" (Eph. 2:4)
- "rich in faith" (James 2:5)
- "riches of His kindness" (Romans 2:4)
- "riches of His glory" (Romans 9:23)

Considering all the many things "rich" can mean in the New Testament, what could "rich" mean in "...that through His poverty you might become rich?" (2 Corinthians 8:9). The sermons I heard could not have made the point more emphatic: "rich means rich" – meaning financially wealthy. My contention with the prosperity teaching is exactly this, that the word is used exclusively to mean material wealth and riches.

Here are reasons why "rich" does *not* mean material wealth in this phrase. First, in the context of chapters 8 and 9 of 2 Corinthians Paul explains the purpose for giving to be *equality* (not the attainment of wealth). Those who had more would share with those who had less, with no one should be left wanting (See 2 Cor. 8:12-15). Meeting others' needs while God meeting the givers' needs wrap up the message of chapters eight and nine of 2 Corinthians.

Second, the Apostle Paul describes his own ministry and its many paradoxes in 2 Corinthians 6:10 using the same expressions as he did to describe Jesus' ministry in 2 Corinthians 8:9.

> "...as unknown, and yet well known; as dying, and behold we live; as chastened, and yet not killed; as sorrowful, yet always rejoicing; *as poor, yet making many rich*; as having nothing, and yet possessing all things." (2 Corinthians 6:9-10, italics added)

By the argument that "rich means rich" one would have to conclude that Paul was making many financially rich. But that is not what Paul meant at all. As he became poor for the Gospel's sake – by leaving everything behind and joining the company of the early disciples, working diligently to support himself, while also receiving donations – he had no money to make others materially rich, and certainly that was not his intention. However, he made many, many rich *in Christ*! As Christ did, he also, through his poverty, made many rich in Christ!

Why would Paul choose to become poor to make others rich in Christ? Because he had come to know too well that earthly riches do not

110

compare with riches in Christ. Jesus brought us something so much greater than earthly riches. Earthly riches not only cannot satisfy but tend to want to take the place of the source of all riches, Jesus Christ. This, I believe, is the reason riches are presented in such unfavorable light in the New Testament. Jesus has come, and He is Supreme. The New Testament presents a shift from the earthly to the Heavenly. But there is still one more proof that "rich" in 2 Corinthians 8:9 means "rich in Christ" and not in material wealth.

Wealth and Lukewarmness

Revelation 3:14-18 offers, perhaps, the best explanation for the word "rich" in 2 Corinthians 8:9. In this passage Jesus addresses the church at Laodicea, the last of seven churches. Many Bible scholars hold that this church represents and describes part of the church age today. The choice word by Jesus to describe this church is "lukewarm:"

> And to the angel of the church of the Laodiceans write, 'These things says the Amen, the Faithful and True Witness, the Beginning of the creation of God: I know your works, that you are neither cold nor hot. I could wish you were cold or hot. So then, because *you are lukewarm*, and neither cold nor hot, I will vomit you out of My mouth (Revelation 3:14-16, italics added)

What caused them to become lukewarm? Here is Jesus' answer:

> "*Because* you say, '*I am rich, have become wealthy, and have need of nothing*'—and do not know that you are wretched, miserable, poor, blind, and naked— I counsel you to *buy from Me* gold refined in the fire, that *you may be rich*; and white garments, that you may be clothed, that the shame of your nakedness may not be revealed; and anoint your eyes with eye salve, that you may see. (Revelation 3:17-18, NKJV, italics added)

Unmistakably, Jesus connects wealth and the associated fulfillment with lukewarmness. The reason for this can be best explained by the

111

Beatitudes in Luke's account – the blessings and woes. Blessed are the poor for they hunger for those things pertaining to Christ; woe to those who are satisfied. Wealth, comfort, and pleasures, by satisfying the flesh, tend to either squelch or mask deeper soul and spiritual hunger – that is, one's need for Christ. Earthly satisfaction can produce spiritual "wretched(ness), miserable(ness), poor (poverty), blind(ness), and naked(ness)." It is like the present comfort blinds the individual to see more, far more than he could experience or even imagine, on earth.

The phrase "that you may be rich" obviously means "rich in Christ," and we can deduce it means the same as in 2 Corinthians 8:9: "that...you might become rich."

Revelation 3:17-18 is obviously talking about two kinds of riches. One is earthly and the other is heavenly. Christ came to bring heavenly riches while warning against storing up and pursuing earthly riches. *Pursuing* wealth, especially without direction from God, compromises a Christian's wholehearted and single-minded devotion to Christ and His kingdom. This causes him to become lukewarm.

If Jesus emphasized heavenly riches and cautioned pursuing earthly riches, how did He live? Was He rich or poor? Some teachers argue that Jesus and His disciples were rich – namely, that they had much earthly possession and lived a rich lifestyle. This would have to be so to justify the position that it is God's will for us all to be wealthy and to live a luxurious lifestyle. It would be strange for a Christ follower to pursue prosperity (riches and wealth) if Jesus and His disciples were either poor or chose to remain poor for any reason. To establish whether Jesus was rich or poor is rather important.

Was Jesus Rich or Poor?

Jesus taught much about the poor and the rewards to those who give to them. A reward Jesus emphasized for giving to the poor was treasures in heaven. In the sermon on the mount, long before He advised the rich young ruler to sell everything he had and give it to the poor, He taught the crowd to do the same. In the parallel passages of Matthew 6:19-34, and Luke 12:22-34, Luke adds this verse, 33: "Sell what you possess and give donations to the poor; provide yourselves with purses and handbags that do not grow old, an unfailing and inexhaustible treasure in the heavens, where not thief comes near and no moth destroys," and continues: "For where your treasure is, there will your heart be also." (34, Amp.) There is great reward awaiting those who give to the poor. It is interesting to note that the story of the rich young ruler is included in three Gospels - Matthew, Mark, and Luke. Not many parables or sayings of Jesus are recorded in three Gospels. It must be very important to God.

The question may arise, did Jesus Himself give to the poor? Was Jesus an example for all to follow, or was He just a teacher who told them what to do? Was Jesus ever rich on earth? Second Corinthians 8:9 says, "He became poor." When did He become poor? How did He become poor? Does it refer to spiritual poverty, such as leaving the comfort of His Father and hosts of angels, or to earthly, material poverty? If this poverty refers to earthly, material, poverty, was He poor during His whole lifetime on earth, or did He start out rich and became poor later? If He became poor later, was it on the cross after having enjoyed a rich lifestyle, as some teach, or, by giving away everything He acquired during his life, as He instructed His disciples to do?

From the biblical account we gather that the offerings Mary brought at Jesus' baby dedication point to the possibility that she and Joseph were not wealthy. At this celebration, the Law required that she brings a lamb and a young pigeon or turtle dove (Leviticus 12:6). However, "if she is not able to bring a lamb, then she may bring two turtledoves or two young pigeons—one as a burnt offering and the other as a sin offering..." (Leviticus 12:8). From Luke 2:22-24 we gather that she presented two birds, indicating that they could not afford a lamb.

However, Jesus likely acquired great wealth when He was still very young. Wise men from the East brought Him gold, frankincense, and myrrh – very expensive gifts fit for a king. We do not know how many wise men came, the Bible does not tell us, but historically wise men traveled in large crowds of dozens and possibly over a hundred. Small numbers were in much danger from robbers, especially traveling long distances. So, Jesus may have acquired great wealth from these wise men. If He was wealthy, did His life indicate a luxurious, wealthy lifestyle fit for a king?

I believe that He came among us to teach us the right way to live and to exemplify what He taught. If Jesus had not practiced what He preached, He would have been a hypocrite. When Jesus preached healing, He healed. When He preached forgiveness, He forgave. When He preached "give to the poor," He gave (see John 13:27-29). He likely gave away most everything He had to the poor and became poor Himself. When He preached "do not store up treasures on earth," that is what He did. He used His poverty to teach dependence on and faith in God. So, when He instructed His disciples to live by faith, He had to show them how.

How could He teach confidently to not worry about what we shall eat, or drink, or put on, if He did not live it Himself and show by His example how to trust His Father for those things? He trusted the Father not only for Himself but taught the disciples to trust the Father for themselves and even to meet others' needs. When evening had come after Jesus taught and healed many one day, the disciples urged Jesus to send the throng away to buy food for themselves. Jesus' reply astonished the disciples. He said: "...*you* give them something to eat." (Matthew 14:16, italics added). There were 5000 men plus women and children! If Jesus taught living by faith, He had to have faith to demonstrate and to live by.

Therefore, if He started life rich, to remain rich and live a luxurious lifestyle, He would have had to violate all His teachings on selling what you have, giving it to the poor, and not storing up treasures on earth. Jesus did not only give to the poor, but by becoming poor, He totally identified Himself with them. The most sobering Scripture in the entire New Testament is Matthew 25:34-46. This sums up better than any other Scripture God's heart for the poor, and the consequences for helping or not helping them:

> 34 Then the King will say to those on His right hand, 'Come, you blessed of My Father, inherit the kingdom prepared for you from the foundation of the world: 35 for I was hungry and you gave Me food; I was thirsty and you gave Me drink; I was a stranger and you took Me in; 36 I was naked and you clothed Me; I was sick and you visited Me; I was in prison and you came to Me.'

> 37 "Then the righteous will answer Him, saying, 'Lord, when did we see You hungry and feed You, or thirsty and give You drink? 38 When did we see You a stranger and take You in, or naked and clothe You? 39 Or when did we see You sick, or in prison, and come to You?' 40 And the King will answer and say to them, 'Assuredly, I say to you, inasmuch as you did it to one of the least of these My brethren, you did it to Me.'

> 41 "Then He will also say to those on the left hand, 'Depart from Me, you cursed, into the everlasting fire prepared for the devil and his angels: 42 for I was hungry and you gave Me no food; I was thirsty and you gave Me no drink; 43 I was a stranger and you did not take Me in, naked and you did not clothe Me, sick and in prison and you did not visit Me.'

> 44 "Then they also will answer Him, saying, 'Lord, when did we see You hungry or thirsty or a stranger or naked or sick or in prison, and did not minister to You?' 45 Then He will answer them, saying, 'Assuredly, I say to you, inasmuch as you did not do it to one of the least of these, you did not do it to Me.' 46 And these will go away into everlasting punishment, but the righteous into eternal life."

In pondering the question whether He actually had things to give up or sacrifice, I believe that just as the wise men lavished Him with expensive gifts and Mary Magdalene poured very expensive perfume over Him, many who recognized Him may have brought Him gifts untold. As a Jew, the many promises of the Old Testament applied to Him that would have guaranteed financial and other successes and blessings in His life, such as the blessings we read about in Deuteronomy 28.

We do not really know much about Jesus' personal life from the Scriptures, as His life on earth was not about Him, but about others. We can surmise from His teachings that He was not worried about what He was going to eat or drink, or what clothes He was going to wear, but that He focused purely on establishing God's Kingdom on earth. He may or may not have had a house, but we do know that He was on the road so much to preach the kingdom of God that He told a potential follower: "Foxes have holes and the birds of the air have lodging places, but the Son of Man has nowhere to lay His head." (Matthew 8:20)

Should He have kept all the riches and gifts He received, He could have likely become very rich. But He considered others more important than Himself and likely gave away everything He had.

While God's plan for His people in the Old Testament was to increase in possessions, His plan for Jesus and His disciples was to "Go into all the world and preach the Gospel to every creature" (Mark 16:15), to give freely and to live by faith. With this mandate came God's promise that He would supply all the needs of those who thus live.

Does God Want Us Poor?

Based on everything presented so far, one may sincerely ask: "Does God expect His followers to be poor?" God's original plan was never for any of his children to lack anything. Poverty came with the curse. The idea that God would want us poor contradicts all admonitions in the Scriptures to help the poor. If God would want us poor, Christ would not have given His life to free us from poverty and other forms of oppression. Poverty is a state of lack of basic necessities and God does not desire that for any of His creation.

On the contrary, the creation story reminds us of God's effusive plan. He created the earth with its stunning beauty and vast resources and then gave it to man to enjoy and exercise dominion over it. The wealth of the earth is not designated to the few select but to everyone. He never intended for some to lavish in wealth while others have nothing. He made this clear when He distributed the Promised Land among the tribes. Deuteronomy 15:4 says: "But *there will be no poor among you*, for the Lord will surely bless you in the land which the Lord your God gives you for an inheritance to possess." (Italics added). Note the second half of the verse that explains why there should be no poor among them: "for the Lord will surely bless you...." There is no excuse or reason for the poor to be when God abundantly provides.

Poverty is the result of the curse which entered the world through disobedience. The enemy of our souls reigns in this world and through greed the poor get poorer while the rich get richer. The poor in the Scriptures describe people who are oppressed, exploited, vulnerable and weak. Under the Old Covenant God instituted laws to protect them. He instituted the second tithe, the year of release every seventh year (Deuteronomy 15), and the year of Jubilee. The year of Jubilee represented every 50th year when God restored all things He originally gave His people – freedom and inheritances.

This provision by God, in particular, protected many from becoming forever slaves and forever poor. The year of Jubilee helped halt the natural progression of wealth and power redistribution, whereby the rich were getting richer and the poor poorer. In addition to these ordinances, God presented many opportunities for free-will offerings for the poor. His heart is well expressed in the following passage:

> 7 If there is among you a poor man, one of your kinsmen in any of the towns of your land which the Lord your God gives you, you shall not harden your [minds and] hearts or close your hands to your poor brother; 8 But you shall open your hands wide to him and shall surely lend him sufficient for his need in whatever he lacks. 9 Beware lest there be a base thought in your [minds and] hearts, and you say, The seventh year, the year of release, is at hand, and your eye be evil against your poor brother and you give him nothing, and he cry to the Lord against you, and it be sin in you. 10 You shall give to him freely without begrudging it; because of this the Lord will bless you in all your work and in all you undertake. 11 For the poor will never cease out of the land; **therefore I command you, You shall open wide your hands to your brother, to your needy, and to your poor in your land.** (Deuteronomy 15:7-11, Amp) (Emphasis added)

Jesus came to deliver the oppressed from their oppression and oppressors. Poverty is one form of oppression. Since we are battling against strong spiritual forces, abolishing poverty may be out of our reach, but helping the poor whenever, wherever, and however we can is fulfilling God's heart. This is so strong with God that He personalized giving to the poor as giving to Him several times in the Scriptures. One is the example of Jesus whom we just quoted as saying "Inasmuch as ye have done it unto one of the least of these my brethren, ye have done it unto me." Jesus so identifies Himself with the poor that giving to the poor means the same as giving to Him.

A similar identification takes place with the tithe. God says the tithe belongs to Him, but then He qualifies that it belongs to the Levites, orphans, widows, and foreigners. When His children are not taken care of, He takes it personally. His reputation is at stake. He promised to provide, but He designed it so that He provides through us.

Scripturally, we should not take lightly using the phrases "belongs to God" and "giving to God." Scripturally, giving to God means giving to the poor and needy. God does not want anyone to be in lack or in want. So, does God want us poor? Naturally, not! However, He invites some of us to a life of faith where we *choose to* give up comfort and an easy life for the sake of the gospel and follow Jesus.

Does God Want Us Wealthy?

God does not want us poor, but does He want us wealthy? Undoubtedly, God's original plan was to lavish His children with all the wealth and riches of this world. Sin, however marred the hearts of men, and the enemy of our soul, satan, has come to steal, kill, and destroy. In spite of this, God's plan for His children is abundance, at least having all sufficiency for all things.

In the New Testament great caution is expressed against wealth and riches because of its strong capacity to lure men into following it, rather than the Lord Jesus. "But those who desire to be rich fall into temptation and a snare, and into many foolish and harmful lusts which drown men in destruction and perdition" (1 Timothy 6:9). So, Jesus would say, "if your right hand causes you to sin, cut it off and cast it from you; for it is more profitable for you that one of your members perish, than for your whole body to be cast into hell." (Matthew 5:30) In other words, if one is tempted to pursue riches at the expense of following Christ, it is better for them to live under humble circumstances and hunger after God, than having much material possessions and reject God.

Expressions of God that He wants His children to be rich and wealthy are not found in the New Testament as in the Old. That does not mean, however, that God does not want some of us to make much money or that wealth should not come to us today. I believe that the parable of the talents is one example of this in Matthew 25:14-30. The talent refers to money (verse 27). We learn from this parable that Jesus was extremely pleased with the ones who multiplied their money and furious with the one who would not as much as put it in the bank to earn interest but instead hid it in the ground.

When the heart is right, God is not against us making money. In fact, this parable implies that God calls some of us to make more than others, and not stewarding that responsibility may be disobeying God. Making money depends on resources (talents), callings, and abilities. The more one is endowed with these components, the more he can make. One cannot expect the person with the one talent in the parable to make ten talents like his counterpart who received five talents to start with—likewise with the one given two talents. But Jesus did not expect Him to produce ten talents. He was only called to steward what he was given, according to his ability.

We all have something to work with, but we have a choice in the matter. The person with the one talent chose not to do anything with it, not even as much as putting it in the bank to earn some interest. This was not acceptable to Jesus. He wants us to be responsible and to honor Him. Obedience, acceptance of God's sovereign will, contentment, faith, diligence and hard work contribute to how much we will have. Accepting lack and poverty due to laziness is not an option. We need to do the very best we can, not only for our sakes, but for the sake of the kingdom to be able to help those who are truly in need. The call of the prosperity gospel to gain riches in order to support God's kingdom is correct, but there is more to gaining riches than to sow for it, as this parable well explains.

Laziness Debunked

We were created to work. As such, the Bible calls out laziness. Not working is never an option. Love demands that we don't become a burden to others. The great Apostle Paul said this:

7 For you yourselves know how you ought to follow us, for we were not disorderly among you; 8 nor did we eat anyone's bread free of charge, but worked with labor and toil night and day, that we might not be a burden to any of you, 9 not because we do not have authority, but to make ourselves an example of how you should follow us.

10 For even when we were with you, we commanded you this: If anyone will not work, neither shall he eat. 11 For we hear that there are some who walk among you in a disorderly manner, not working at all, but are busybodies. 12 Now those who are such we command and exhort through our Lord Jesus Christ that they work in quietness and eat their own bread. (2 Thessalonians 3:7-12)

The Bible nowhere suggests supporting those who can provide for themselves and running a welfare state. The Scriptures do not advocate laziness, as quoted earlier: "If anyone will not work, neither shall he eat." (2 Thessalonians 3:10). On the contrary, it urges us to work hard to be able to help those who are truly in need. The needy includes our own family first. As the tithe was partly designated for orphans and widows, it follows that one's obligation is to provide for his own family first, or else his children will be like orphans and widows – uncared-for. Not providing for one's own family by not working doesn't rest well with God: "If anyone fails to provide for his relatives, and especially for those of his own family, he has disowned the faith [by failing to accompany it with fruits] and is worse than an unbeliever [who performs his obligation in these matters]." (1 Timothy 5:8 Amp.)

In addition, advancing the kingdom of God requires much of our support – supporting workers and funding ministries. Helping the kingdom advance and helping others begin with taking care of ourselves. As Jesus reiterated that we must love others *as we love ourselves*, it follows that the most loving thing we can do is to take care of and provide for *ourselves* so that we are not a burden to others. We are responsible for our own welfare. May we be ones who give rather than ones who take!

Is Wealth Automatically Guaranteed to Christians?

The prosperity gospel conveys the idea that wealth is guaranteed to Christians by only sowing for it, since Abraham's blessing of wealth is passed down to us through His Seed, Christ Jesus. Is this a correct interpretation of the Abrahamic Covenant?

First, not even in the Old Testament do we see such guarantee. The Old Testament promises of blessings – part of which were wealth and riches – came in context of an Old Covenant relationship with God. These blessings were contingent on obedience to His laws and precepts. "Blessed is the man *who fears the Lord,* Who *delights greatly in His commandments*...Wealth and riches will be in his house." (Psalm 112:1-3, italics added). With wealth came responsibility.

Pursuing wealth without following God's moral laws – the blessings without obedience – is out of order in God's kingdom and is akin to idolatry. When the Israelites disobeyed and rebelled against God's laws and ordinances, they eventually lost all their possessions and even their land when they got driven out of the Promised Land. Still today, part of the most destitute in our world are some of the misplaced Jews living in oppressive countries. Thankfully, many are making their way back to their homeland, Israel. Wealth is not automatically guaranteed.

Second, the promised blessing of Abraham in Christ is not riches, as is taught from Galatians 3:14, but the Holy Spirit and salvation in Christ.

> I will make you a great nation; I will bless you and make your name great; And you shall be a blessing. I will bless those who bless you, And I will curse him who curses you; And in you all the families of the earth shall be blessed. (Genesis 12: 2-3)

> Christ has redeemed us from the curse of the law, having become a curse for us (for it is written, "Cursed is everyone who hangs on a tree"), that the blessing of Abraham might come upon the Gentiles *in Christ Jesus, that we might receive the promise of the Spirit through faith.* (Galatians 3: 13-14, italics added)

Let us read the last verse again: "that the blessing of Abraham might come upon the Gentiles *in Christ Jesus.*" The promised blessing of Abraham to all the families of the earth and to the Gentiles is not *in* financial prosperity but *in Christ Jesus* and the accompanying promised *Holy Spirit* whom we receive through faith! (Like Abraham received his promise through faith.) Verse 16 further explains:

> "Now to Abraham and his Seed were the promises made. He does not say, 'And to seeds,' as of many, but as of one, 'And to your Seed,' who is Christ."

The promise was not made to many individuals to make them rich, but to the *one* Seed, Christ, *in whom* is the promise fulfilled: salvation offered to all men through Him and the Holy Spirit through faith.

Earthly Poverty for Heavenly Riches

Just as we get to choose here on earth how much money we desire to make, it is up to us how much treasure and rewards we want to build in our permanent future place – Heaven. Jesus does not tell us; it is up to us. The decision boils down to how much comfort, pleasure, ease, power, and prestige we want to experience in this life and how much of these we are willing to let go. Most of us seem to hang onto some level of comfort. Giving up things for God may come back to us here on earth, but most likely in heaven.

Just to think how much treasure the rich young ruler gave up in heaven when he refused to sell his possessions and give the money to the poor! He would not have become destitute, for God promised to supply the needs of those who are generous (Philippians 4:19, 2 Cor. 8:12-15).

123

Promises of rewards are wonderful motivators but the road is hard. God's main quest is the souls of men. The Apostle Paul urged us "to become all things to all men for the sake of the Gospel" (1 Corinthians 9:19-23). Becoming all things to all men may mean for some to become rich and to reach those in that stratum of society, but for many others it may mean living under humble circumstances. Jesus and many of the disciples chose that road.

The question, "Does God want us wealthy?" takes on a new perspective. Yes, He wants us to be "good and faithful" in multiplying our resources (parable of the talents) so we can have much. No, He does not want us to hoard, or "build bigger barns" as did the rich man in Jesus' following parable:

> 16 Then He spoke a parable to them, saying: "The ground of a certain rich man yielded plentifully. 17 And he thought within himself, saying, 'What shall I do, since I have no room to store my crops?' 18 So he said, 'I will do this: I will pull down my barns and build greater, and there I will store all my crops and my goods. 19 And I will say to my soul, "Soul, you have many goods laid up for many years; take your ease; eat, drink, and be merry."' 20 But God said to him, 'Fool! This night your soul will be required of you; then whose will those things be which you have provided?' 21 "So is he who lays up treasure for himself, and is not rich toward God." (Luke 12)

In today's world, his crops could represent God's blessings financially. The increase in money is followed by an increase in purchases. With the growing number of goods, the need arises for bigger or more houses to make room for all new gadgets, furniture, and whatever else one deems valuable. Yet when death comes, one cannot take any one of those items with them. I believe this scenario describes a good percent of believers today. Interestingly, Jesus followed this parable with:

> 22 Then He said to His disciples, "Therefore I say to you, do not worry about your life, what you will eat; nor about the body, what you will put on....

Taking care of the needy, and one another, is what being in Christ is about. Christ feels the pain of the poor, and so should we. "If a brother or sister is naked and destitute of daily food, and one of you says to them, 'Depart in peace, be warmed and filled,' but you do not give them the things which are needed for the body, what does it profit?" (James 2:15-16).

The truly rich person is the one who is rich toward others, and therefore, rich toward God. Christ is the epitome of giving it all. He laid down His life; He made Himself completely poor. It's up to us how far we want to go. There is no condemnation from God to us; He loves us the same. May He show us His way for us on this path and bless us with discernment as to where and to whom He wants us to give.

Tithing for Gain

On a last note, in the teaching I was exposed to, acquiring wealth *to* fund kingdom work was a common theme and a basis for encouraging the flock to tithe and give in order to gain more. However, since wealth was associated with being blessed by God, some people would find themselves investing more money in "looking" wealthy than in helping the needy or advancing the kingdom of God, even if the promised blessings of increase were not materialized. The pressure was so great (yet subtle) to look "blessed" that some people would borrow money to buy a newer car, a bigger house, newer wardrobe, or other wealthy looking things. The focus in this doctrine, clearly, shifts from others to self – a sure sign that this teaching does not reflect the Spirit of the New Testament.

To give should be a major aspiration. Where we give and who we give to matters to God. As one example, "He who oppresses the poor to increase his riches, And he who gives to the rich, will surely come to poverty." (Proverbs 22:6)

We are to follow the Apostle Paul's kind exhortation: "Set your mind on things above, not on things on the earth." (Colossians 3:2) Not understanding that giving brings us treasures primarily in heaven, we may be disappointed and disillusioned when we are not seeing the expected results. Paul's example should put us on the right track.

He gave his life to preach the Gospel, and actively collected funds for the poor brothers and sisters undergoing persecution. Even if he did not have much to give – after all, we know that he was working on the side as a tentmaker to make ends meet - he mobilized others to give, which would have earned him great rewards. Yet, he testified thus: "To the present hour we both hunger and thirst, and we are poorly clothed, and beaten, and homeless." (1 Cor. 4:11)

Instead of fighting his poverty, he learned to be content: "Not that I speak in regard to need, for I have learned in whatever state I am, to be content: I know how to be abased, and I know how to abound. Everywhere and in all things I have learned both to be full and to be hungry, both to abound and to suffer need." (Philippians 4:11-12)

Here is where the prosperity gospel breaks down. The prosperity gospel preaches gain in riches on earth. The Bible preaches gain in godliness with contentment. "Now godliness with contentment is great gain." (1 Timothy 6:6). With that thought and the following assuring Word from the book of Hebrews we end this chapter:

> Let your character or moral disposition be free from love of money [including greed, avarice, lust, and craving for earthly possessions] and be satisfied with your present [circumstances and with what you have]; for He [God] Himself has said, *I will not in any way fail you nor give you up nor leave you without support. [I will] not, [I will] not, [I will] not in any degree leave you helpless nor forsake nor let [you] down (relax My hold on you)! [Assuredly not!]* (Hebrews 13:5, AMPC, italics added)

AMEN!

126

CONCLUSION

This book studied all the passages on the tithe and commonly taught giving and prosperity passages in their biblical contexts. It brought to light God's heart for giving – His purposes, directives and promises. His message is clear.

God loves us deeply and His heart goes out especially toward the "least of these." Who are the "least of these?" In a spiritual sense, we all are them, having been born into sin and hopeless without God. In His love, God reached out to us to save us from our misery. Before the final redemption could be accomplished through Jesus Christ, God did not desert or forsake His special creation who had fallen into sin. He chose to tabernacle among them while He taught them how to stay connected with Him.

Connection involved numerous animal sacrifices to atone for sins. The Levitical tribe was chosen to help with these sacrifices, and due to their full-time service in the Tabernacle, the Levites received tithes from the other tribes as their inheritance, while the other tribes received land. A fair exchange was made: food for service. The tithe was very specific in its designation and purpose. In every instance when the Bible talks about the tithe, it refers to this tithe under the Law of Moses, apart from Abraham's and Jacob's vow. There is no other tithe or tithing mentioned in the Bible.

When Jesus offered Himself as the final, perfect sacrifice, He forever destroyed the power of sin over us and no more sacrifices were needed to be offered. With His resurrection He ushered in the New Covenant and abolished the Old, bringing to an end the Mosaic Law and the Mosaic tithe. No more is tithing, or a principle of tenth pertaining to giving, mentioned in the New Testament for the born-again believers. If not the principle of "tenth" then what principle are we to follow?

The spirit of the tithe – the heart of giving that made sure that people were fed – continues into the New Covenant. The tithe was food for the Levites who did not get land for inheritance. They were supplied through the tithe. A second tithe provided food at the Feasts of celebration, and food for the poor in one's town. Giving in the New Testament is also directed to the poor and to those who are called to full time ministry.

Jesus calls the "least of these" His "brethren" (Matthew 25:40) who are: the destitute, the poor, the persecuted, and those in prison. His heart is so interconnected with them that He declares giving to them is the same as giving to Him. The phrase "giving to God" applies to these, as well as those engaged in kingdom work, according to both the biblical tithe of the Old Testament and New Testament teachings.

If God wants to help the poor, then He certainly would not want to put a burden on them and on those struggling to make ends meet. The Mosaic tithe helped the poor and needy. That cannot be said about paying tenth of income, which is applied across the board to everyone. Paying tenth of income can be oppressive to the poor – putting a demand on them that they may not be able to meet. A high-income earner may easily be able to give away 50 percent or more of their income without significantly affecting their standard of living, while a very low-income earner may have to face parting with basic needs in order to give away ten percent of his or her income.

The Father imposes no specific amount to give in the New Covenant. Giving is not measured in percent of income, but according to (1) what one has, and not according to what one does not have (2 Cor. 8:12); (2) what is in one's heart and given cheerfully and without compulsion; and (3) is given generously or sacrificially.

No doubt, giving ensures a person of great rewards, but not of earthly riches, but of treasures in heaven. While God promised to supply abundantly the needs of those who give generously – He certainly would not want any of His children to lack any basic need – His promised rewards are primarily heavenly: storing up riches in heaven and not on earth. The concept that we are to give money to gain an abundant financial harvest – to become rich and wealthy – finds no support or evidence in the New Testament. Pursuing riches for earthly gain is antithetical to everything Jesus and the apostles preached and exemplified.

God honors riches gained through wisdom, hard work, and His blessings. However, the Bible warns us against storing up riches on earth. The blessing of increase is that there is more to give away. As we give, God continues to bless. To hoard is antithetical not only to the outright command – to not store up riches on earth -- but to the Spirit of Christ, whose heart is to give. James asked this question: "If a brother or sister is naked and destitute of daily food, and one of you says to them, 'Depart in peace, be warmed and filled,' but you do not give them the things which are needed for the body, what does it profit?" (James 2:15-16)

Prosperity is certainly God's will for us; however, biblical prosperity begins with the soul (3 John 2) and is primarily experienced in the soul and spirit. It does not exclude riches when God so blesses, but riches do not encompass or replace prosperity of soul and spirit, to which the Bible alludes.

Before we conclude, some might feel that an important discussion was missing – that of giving to the church. The Scriptures that took center stage in this study did not mention giving to a church or organization. In these passages, giving was always mentioned in context of meeting individual needs, however, that would not exclude giving to churches and ministries. Kingdom work is best accomplished in unity.

Building His kingdom is God's top priority. What is His kingdom? It is His children walking in righteousness, peace and joy on earth (Romans 14:17). It is His children who love, build up, encourage, teach, comfort, and take care of one another, and who draw and teach others to do the same. The kingdom is about love. It is about relationship. Out of the heart, applying wisdom, and guided by God's Holy Spirit we give – generously, cheerfully, not grudgingly or out of compulsion.

May we be filled with His Spirit and find the help we need to express God's grace, mercy and love to one another. May we bask in His unfailing love! May we be free to give from our hearts, consider others more important than ourselves, and keep the Kingdom of God in front of our eyes!